JULES VERNE: THE MAN WHO INVENTED THE FUTURE

BY FRANZ BORN

Translated from the German by Juliana Biro

SCHOLASTIC BOOK SERVICES
New York Toronto London Auckland Sydney Tokyo

Original German title:
Der Mann der die Zukunft erfand

ISBN: 0-590-02379-9

17 16 15 14 13 12 11 10 9 8 7   9/7 01/8

Printed in the U.S.A.

06

Books by Jules Verne

* TWENTY THOUSAND LEAGUES UNDER THE SEA
* THE MYSTERIOUS ISLAND
* JOURNEY TO THE CENTER OF THE EARTH
* FROM THE EARTH TO THE MOON
* AROUND THE WORLD IN EIGHTY DAYS
FIVE WEEKS IN A BALLOON
MICHAEL STROGOFF
THE GREEN RAY
AT THE NORTH POLE
DOCTOR OX'S EXPERIMENT
MASTER OF THE WORLD
INTO THE ABYSS
OFF ON A COMET
THE UNWILLING DICTATOR
PURCHASE OF THE NORTH POLE
AMONG THE CANNIBALS

*Available in Scholastic Book Services editions.

CONTENTS

1 THE FATHER OF MODERN SCIENCE FICTION

THE TREMENDOUS SOLITUDE of the Arctic Ocean was suddenly broken when a huge submarine rose to the surface. Immediately afterward it cut through the gray-green waves on its rapid journey.

It was 9:57 A.M., New York time, August 5, 1958.

In precisely eighty-seven hours and seventeen minutes the U. S. Navy's atomic submarine *Nautilus* had traveled the entire distance beneath the polar ice cap from the West, and had thereby created a new water route between the Pacific and the Atlantic oceans. The experiment, a most carefully guarded secret, had proven successful, and the last corner of the earth had been explored!

Captain William R. Anderson and his officers stood proudly on deck while the news of their adventurous journey under water — a trip of some 1,830 miles — was broadcast to the entire world by radio.

The press of the world acclaimed the *Nautilus* and its courageous crew. At the same time, the world honored a man long dead — Jules Verne. Once again the name of this great storyteller circled the world. Once more one of his technical fantasies had become a fact.

Almost a hundred years before the *Nautilus* was launched, millions of Jules Verne's readers had been enthralled by a mysterious submarine which its author had christened the *Nautilus.* This fictional submarine was able to remain under water for any desired length of time and was likely to make a sudden appearance anywhere in the seven seas.

The *Nautilus* was created in the days when people were still crossing the ocean in steamers that carried a full set of sails, and traveling by train was the same as risking your life. At that time, gaslight was still considered a luxury and electricity was known only to scientists. Yet, Jules Verne's submarine *Nautilus* roamed the depths of the Atlantic, the Pacific, and the Indian oceans in a novel with the exciting title *Twenty Thousand Leagues Under the Sea.*

This book, which immediately became a sensational success, appeared in the year 1869, and it is still being read today.

The novel was, and still is, remarkable because it foreshadowed to an astonishing degree many inventions of the future such as diving chambers, air conditioning, oxygen tanks, electric measuring devices, and most fantastic of all, the *Nautilus* itself

The extraordinary thing about its French storyteller, who in the last century created modern science fiction, is the fact that all the technological inventions he described in his novels were soon to be "discovered" by scientists. No wonder his readers called Jules Verne "the man who invented the future."

Among his millions of readers were young people of all classes and countries, as well as scientists, artists, and even rulers such as the Pope, the Czar, the King of England, and Emperor William II, who once called Jules Verne his favorite author.

At a time when the conquest of the air appeared utterly impossible to his contemporaries, Jules Verne was presenting his readers with the experience of flying and envisioning the helicopter. In his eighty-odd novels, almost all published before 1900, we find examples of remote control aviation, modern armaments, the talking motion picture, television, synthetic materials, a space rocket with live animals aboard, and the experience of flying at supersonic speeds. Verne even described the atomic bomb and gave full details of a trip to the moon, manned by scientists.

And what we read in his *Diary of an American Journalist of the Year 2850* is even today still a dream of the future. Here Verne describes a world-capital with rolling sidewalks and advertising that is projected into the clouds. He speaks of the television-telephone, television news reporting from Mars and Jupiter, and a single vehicle which will serve as an airplane, an automobile, or a motor-boat.

Jules Verne's "inventions" fascinated his fans — but few took them seriously. When he died in 1905, a Paris newspaper said: "The old storyteller is dead. Is it not as if Santa Claus has died?"

But a small group of inventors and explorers were already at work to make the "fairy tales" of this "Santa Claus" come true. Many famous scientists have publicly acknowledged that they were inspired by Jules Verne's science fiction.

When Simon Lake, a twelve-year-old American boy, read Jules Verne's novel *Twenty Thousand Leagues Under the Sea,* he vowed that one day he would build a submarine like the *Nautilus* and travel under the seven seas like the author's Captain Nemo. Thirty years later he had realized his ambition; his submarine had become the *Nautilus* piece by piece.

Admiral Byrd, who conquered both poles from the air and who became the great explorer of the Antarctic, told newsmen before setting out on his third great expedition to the South Pole that it was Jules Verne who had brought him there. As a boy he had read Verne's *The Adventures of Captain Hatteras*, and ever since had wanted to conquer the Pole.

Not only the technical inventions envisioned and described by Jules Verne, but also the extraordinary voyages and expeditions on which he allowed many of his heroes to embark, were later realized. And here we encounter something very remarkable indeed. So many details, which are now historic facts, remind us of scenes from Jules Verne's novels.

Jules Verne described the conquest of the North Pole forty-five years before Captain Peary was actually to set foot there. The race between two nations for the conquest of the Pole, which Jules Verne described in *The Adventures of Captain Hatteras*, actually took place in 1911, when the Norwegian Roald Amundsen and the Englishman Robert F. Scott vied with one another to be the first to reach the South Pole.

Norbert Casteret, one of the great pioneers in modern cave exploration, has written: "It was

Jules Verne who encouraged me to penetrate the great caves in the Pyrenees."

In 1948, the world-famous Swiss oceanographer Auguste Piccard first plumbed the depths of the ocean near the Cape Verde Islands in his new diving bell, the bathysphere. Piccard later wrote that the panorama that unfolded before him seemed like a scene out of *Twenty Thousand Leagues Under the Sea*, which he had read as a boy.

The fabulous career of Jules Verne began in 1863, when his first book, entitled *Five Weeks in a Balloon*, caused a sensation. It describes an adventurous balloon journey over the interior of Africa, which was then still completely unknown. In this age of our great-grandparents, Verne's book had the effect of a kind of bombshell. It was something completely new and unheard of which had appeared among all the popular romantic novels.

Here was a book dealing with technology and with the conquest of nature through technology, which had as its hero a completely unromantic, matter-of-fact man, with an adventurous spirit and a cool head on his shoulders. This was the hero of tomorrow, the hero of the dawning scientific era.

Five Weeks in a Balloon was soon translated into all the major languages of the world, and people on both sides of the Atlantic waited impatiently for another book by this new author.

What sort of a person was this Jules Verne,

with his unusual ideas? Where would one go looking for this man, who could imagine the most improbable adventures in the fields of technology
and science? Among the engineers, perhaps, or
among the scientists?

Not at all! One would find the twenty-one-year-
old author in a garret in the artists' quarter in Paris
trying to make a living as a playwright!

How it came about that Jules Verne wrote his
first famous novel is a novel in itself. It is the story
of a young man who felt that he was destined to
achieve something of importance but did not know
how to go about it. It is the ever-fascinating story
of a great man whose destiny leads him through
detours and failures to the final realization of his
talents.

The story of Jules Verne's quest begins about
1840 in the small French seaport town of Nantes.
He was twelve then and walked down to the
docks. He loved to watch the sailboats embark for
distant journeys to far-off lands which he had
never seen — except in his imagination. Jules'
father, a strict and exacting lawyer, could not, for
the life of him, imagine why his son was such a
mediocre student and had no taste at all for his
school assignments. He knew nothing of Jules'
imaginings.

2 THE MAKING OF A WRITER

LIFE IN THE HOME of the lawyer Pierre Verne in Nantes was most correct and punctual.

Every day, at midday and in the evening, Father Verne would check all the clocks and the pocketwatches in the house to make sure that they were keeping correct time. He knew the *exact* distance from his house to his office and had even calculated the number of strides it took him to get there. Unfortunately, Father Verne also knew precisely the distance to the school attended by Jules and his younger brother, Paul, and just how long that walk *should* take, too. Being late for school was an unforgivable offense.

Every evening at 8:30 the two boys said goodnight to their parents. Their father had not the faintest notion that his sons often stayed awake, frequently until dawn, reading travel books by the light of a candle. And when it was too dangerous to light a candle, Jules and Paul would invent a journey to distant lands or even around the whole world, and imagine the most breathtaking adventures on land and sea. Both boys found this pastime much more interesting than their Latin lessons.

In fact, the boys were often not as orderly and punctual as Father Verne might have wished. In the early summer of 1838, Jules and Paul had on several occasions arrived late for supper. Their father soon knew the reason; the two boys had been hanging around the docks again. Their gentle, loving mother had to intervene, as she did so many times, to prevent an overly severe punishment.

But what occurred the following week was indeed without precedent in the history of the Verne family!

One fine afternoon, Jules simply did not come home, and he had not returned home two hours after the usual time. The boy must have met with an accident! Father Verne jumped into the saddle and rode off in search of his son. He went directly to the harbor, and learned at a tavern that Jules had been seen there early that morning. The boy had asked to be rowed out to a three-masted schooner — and this schooner had sailed just half an hour before.

The telegraph — in those days it was still the wooden dial-telegraph — was immediately set in motion. The schooner in question was the *Coralie*, bound for the West Indies, and it was known that it would land once more at a nearby port to take up cargo. Father Verne rode there and personally hauled his stowaway son from his hiding place on the ship.

His father controlled his temper and did not say one word to Jules until they reached home. But then there was a terrible scene in which Father Verne's cane played an important part.

Next day Jules tearfully promised his mother that he would never do anything like that again. From now on he would travel only in his dreams, he assured her. Jules took his promise seriously, but for a long time he mourned his unsuccessful adventure. After a while, his imagination took a completely different direction.

At sixteen, Jules found the romantic poets. Suddenly a whole new world of poetry and theater opened for him. And what a marvelous world it was! Jules immediately began to write a play, to write poetry, and to fall in love with his cousin, to whom he dedicated all his efforts.

During the next few years he appeared to have turned away completely from the sea and distant lands. He now had a new goal, and this was to become a writer and to conquer Paris and all of France with his pen. But how could he get away from Nantes and live in Paris? The opportunity would present itself, as he was to discover, on his twentieth birthday.

Father Verne was pleased to believe that his oldest son, Jules, would study law. Of course, Jules could have studied law in Nantes. Still, Jules' younger brother Paul was leaving home to enter the navy at eighteen, and Father Verne felt that something special should also be arranged for Jules.

Paul would now actually *see* the seven seas and the many foreign lands about which the two brothers had so often dreamed. Jules, on the other hand, was being "treated" to a law course at the Sorbonne in Paris. He was expected to apply himself to his studies with the greatest industry, in order to pass the required examinations and to open his law practice as soon as possible.

How fortunate for Jules that his father had so little imagination, and no inkling of the soaring ambitions and literary dreams of his eldest son.

In the year 1848 there was not yet a railroad connection between Nantes and Paris. On a foggy November morning, the clumsy old mail coach drove into the market place. Jules and his friend Edouard Bonamy had their baggage secured to the roof, bade their families farewell, and rolled away toward their new freedom — which they both planned to enjoy to the hilt.

The two twenty-year-olds arrived in the city of their dreams on a Saturday. It was only a few months after the Revolution of 1848, and they arrived just in time for the celebration of the signing of the new constitution on the *Place de la Concorde*. Bells were ringing everywhere, and the young, romantic poet Jules Verne, with two verse plays in his suitcase, took this to be an exceptionally good omen.

The great adventure had begun!

He took lodgings in an attic room in the Latin Quarter among all the painters, writers, and budding actors. Then young Monsieur Verne betook himself to the Sorbonne, had himself duly registered as a student of law, and immediately afterward left the hallowed halls of the University with the firm intention not to visit them again for the time being. After all, there were good lawyers by the thousands.

It was the Paris of the young Republic that Jules wanted to take by storm as a dramatist — a Paris swarming with elegant coaches, a city of luxury and of the newly rich *bourgeoisie*, where everyone was out to enjoy himself. There were over four hundred ballrooms in the Paris of that gay period, and there were fifty thousand balls given

in four months. The music-loving Jules, who
had loved to dream at the piano, found out that no
less than 133 concerts were to be given during the
winter season, not counting the attractions at the
Grand Opera and the many Parisian theaters.

To one of these theaters he submitted one of the
verse dramas he had brought with him from Nantes, and hoped for luck. The waiting period was
spent on the boulevards, in the cafés, and in the
company of countless new friends from the studios of the Latin Quarter. Everywhere he heard
about the fabulous sums of money that one could
earn as a writer in Paris, if only one could get an
introduction to the editors of the great periodicals.
The most famous authors in those days wrote for
the journals. Eugène Sue had received 100,000
gold francs for his sensational novel *The Eternal
Jew*; Alexandre Dumas had received enough for
his novel *The Count of Monte Cristo* to be able to
build himself a castle in Moorish style with mirror
ceilings and parquet floors, on which lay tiger
skins with gilded claws in place of carpets. What
prospects for his future, thought Jules!

But as the months passed by, Jules gradually
realized that one had to have "connections" in order to sell one's articles, plays or novels, in Paris.
In order to obtain these connections, the young
writer went to the cafes even more frequently,
and had friends take him to social gatherings at

the homes of the newly rich who were always eager to act as patrons to young artists. For a long time the main advantage of these gatherings for Jules Verne lay in the fact that he could eat his fill at the cold buffets, thereby saving the cost of a meal. For he had, of course, spent much more than the allowance he had received from his father, and already had many debts.

He was indeed to make an important acquaintance at one of these gatherings. But first he was to be hit by a veritable thunderclap.

One afternoon there was a knock on the door of his little attic room, and Jules opened it to find himself confronted by — his father. The old gentleman had probably heard rumors about his son's activities. He now cross-examined him with stern thoroughness.

Father Verne could hardly believe what he heard. Jules had not gone to a single lecture at the Sorbonne. Instead, he was hanging around with artists and even had the nerve to be proud of the fact that he had been able to get a play performed at one of the theaters. By his own admission, he spent his days in the restaurants of the Latin Quarter.

Perhaps Father Verne would have let the matter rest with a very severe reprimand, if his son had not rather arrogantly pointed out that an artist in Paris could earn huge sums of money. That was

too much for him. He wished Jules much luck in
earning these huge sums and announced that from
now on he would no longer be sent his monthly
allowance. Only if Jules could prove that he attended his classes regularly would he be able to
count on financial support from home.

This was an unexpected blow! But Jules had no
intention of giving in and studying law. Fate had
better things in store for him, he was certain. His
optimism got the better of his dejection, and for
the time being he still had three hundred francs in
his pocket.

From then on Jules Verne dined regularly on
the cold buffets of bourgeois society. But the
gatherings were usually so boring that he preferred to leave early. And so it happened in an
elegant house on the Faubourg Saint Germain.
Right after the "meal" Jules Verne had departed
unnoticed and stood at the head of the large, luxurious stairway.

The white marble bannister tempted him to
slide down, as he had done so frequently as a
schoolboy. Nobody could see him at that moment,
and so he began a giddy descent on the seat of his
pants. Only too late did he notice that someone
was coming up the stairs. Jules could not stop himself and crashed into a portly gentleman, hitting
him squarely in the stomach! Both fell. Jules
helped his victim up and apologized profusely

and, in his embarrassment, asked with somewhat inappropriate humor:

"I hope you have not yet had your dinner?"

"I most certainly have," replied the portly gentleman. "And it was something especially good: Omelette à la Nantes! And now you have to trample on my belly!"

"From Nantes? What a coincidence," Jules said explaining he was also from Nantes. Jules stuttered sheepishly but managed to say that he could make this dish more expertly than any Parisian chef.

"But then you will have to prepare one for me," the other remarked smilingly. He obviously liked the confused young man. "Come and see me next Monday."

"With pleasure. May I have your address?"

"What? You don't recognize me? I am Alexandre Dumas."

Alexandre Dumas, the successful author of *The Three Musketeers* and *The Count of Monte Cristo*, whose novel *The Queen's Necklace*, published in a huge edition, had just conquered Paris!

From Dumas, the master of the exquisitely constructed novel of suspense, Jules Verne learned the technique of novel-writing. One day his hard schooling would be most useful to him, but for the moment he did not gain anything by it, even if he was able to sell a short story here and there on Dumas' recommendation.

"You must write, write, and write some more,"
his famous friend had preached, "every day at a
set time. It doesn't matter at all whether you pro-
duce anything good or not. But if you keep writing, ideas will come to you."

So, Jules sat down to write punctually at six
each morning. He worked at a table with a drop-
leaf board that served him as a desk. But he was
almost driven to despair. When he wanted to invent one of the historical episodes which were
then so popular, his mind went absolutely blank.
The Middle Ages and the times of Marie Antoin-
ette did not mean anything to him. The love
scenes would not turn out right, and furthermore,
they bored him. When he put down his pen at
noon, he sometimes had produced no more than a
few closely scribbled pages with half of the sen-
tences crossed out.

It was bitter cold in his little attic room. Jules
Verne did not have the money to heat it often. In
fact, he was grateful if he made enough to eat a
warm meal every second day. Gradually, he became very discouraged. He could no longer stand
it in his ice-cold attic and began to roam aimlessly
through the cold dreary streets of Paris. Most of
his friends were in the same financial predicament,
and Jules no longer had the money to sit in a
warm café.

Finally he discovered a refuge — the public li-

braries. There it was warm, it did not cost anything, and furthermore, there were hundreds of
fascinating books which could make one forget
the everyday misery for a few hours. As he had
done in his childhood, the unsuccessful young
writer took up travelogues of all kinds, and in his
imagination he once more fled to the South Seas,
to the Amazon, to the jungles of India, or to the
eternal ice of the North Pole.

That this was a dead end must have been obvious
to him, but he did not want to admit it to himself.
He sat at his desk daily from gray dawn until
noon; then he went to one of the libraries.

Soon the libraries became more important to
him than his laborious hours of work, for in books
he had found a new field which had a strange attraction for him — the natural sciences. He read
volume after volume, and it mattered little whether
it was about botany or zoology, about modern
surveying techniques, about caves, or about new
technological inventions. A new world opened
up before him, which so fascinated him that he
began to take hundreds of notes on little slips of
paper. He was only aroused by the evening bell,
which announced the closing of the library.

The natural sciences — what a huge field! He
read about the heroic deeds of modern engineers
and about the careful calculations that went into
the building of a tunnel or the planning of a new

railroad route. He read about the research being done on the currents of the sea and the secrets of the starry skies. He fled from the everyday into his reading.

He discovered that he had an excellent memory, retaining almost everything he had read. But of what use was this to him at the moment? When he allowed free reign to his technological fantasies, he could imagine himself leading the life of a modern scientist or engineer. He could see himself as an orchid-hunter in the jungles of the Amazon, or as the foreman of a construction team in the midst of a great mountain range. These fantasies were not very different from the dreams of the eleven-year-old boy whose reveries had made him forget his homework. Jules' notes filled a large carton — a veritable treasury of knowledge, for the moment utterly useless to him.

But it is often through such detours from the accepted path that men of genius come to find themselves and the work that they can do best. When judged in the light of the sober, everyday world, what Jules Verne was doing might seem childish and utterly useless. And yet it was exactly at this time that he had reached, all unknowingly, his right path.

Even though he had hardly any time to spare, he did write a few short scientific articles on subjects that were of interest to him at the moment, and sent them to some periodicals for young people, on the chance that they might be accepted. To his great surprise, they were accepted and he was paid fairly well for them. But even so, these fees barely paid his meager expenses for a few days.

He kept on hoping for some turning point, some miracle!

One warm spring day, when Jules had just recuperated sufficiently from a bad case of influenza to dare to go out on the boulevards, he chanced to meet Alexandre Dumas. Dumas, who had just returned from a trip to the Mediterranean, was shocked at the appearance of his young protégé. In his good-natured and helpful way, he aided Jules in obtaining a minor position as a secretary at the *Théâtre Lyrique* in Paris.

A position with a steady salary! Now the worst seemed over.

Jules threw himself enthusiastically into the life of the theater, which had always attracted him like a magnet. He enjoyed rehearsals and the privilege of having an orchestra seat every night, and he especially liked acting in an occasional minor role. But after half a year his first enthusiasm for the theater had vanished. The *Théâtre Lyrique* presented only comic operas and operettas, and Jules often was asked to rewrite the lyrics to make them singable. He found this job even more stultifying than trying to write fashionable novels.

He soon got to know theatrical people so well that he had had enough of them. He learned to despise their unlimited vanity, their petty animosities, and the constant scandals on stage and at rehearsals. But what hit him hardest was the fact that he could not continue to spend those precious hours in the libraries. Instead of exploring the secrets of subterranean caves or studying the planets, he had to write texts for arias and "comic dialogues." Now, it seemed to him, he was hopelessly heading for a dead end.

He stood the life of the theater for four long years, but not without making some unsuccessful attempts at a reconciliation with his father. The elder Verne kept on insisting that Jules study law. His mother occasionally sent him money and counseled him to find a rich wife. He was unable to find a publisher for the few novels he had written during the early morning hours spent at his desk. There would have been reason for despair, if his unshakeable optimism had not always kept him going.

Would it go on like this forever? In order to catch his breath for once and have a little time to think, he sacrificed some of his meager savings in order to take a short vacation. He went to the ocean he loved so much, to Dunkirk. When he returned, Paris was stricken with the cholera, and the *Théâtre Lyrique* had closed its doors for an indefinite period. Once more he was out in the streets.

The colleague who brought Jules the devastating news of the closing of the *Théâtre Lyrique* was in the best of moods because he was just about to make a very advantageous marriage. In order to console Jules a little, his friend, Monsieur Victor, invited him to the wedding as a witness and took him along to Amiens.

The wedding feast lasted for several days. His table partner was a charming young woman called Honorine. She was the bride's older sister. She was only twenty-six years old but already a widow and the mother of two small girls, Valentine and Suzanne. At the end of forty-eight hours Jules Verne was hopelessly in love with her. His affections were reciprocated.

Friend Victor presented Jules to his in-laws as a highly talented young man who had high hopes of success. After one more week Jules was firmly engaged to Honorine. It was only later that he learned that his bride would bring 50,000 *francs* to the marriage.

This meant economic freedom in addition to his happiness. Jules was in seventh heaven. They planned to take a small apartment in Paris, where Jules would have his own attic room. There he could continue his studies alone and undisturbed, and write stories and articles as he wished.

If things could only have been that simple!

Now Father Verne appeared on the scene. He welcomed this marriage, found the bride charming, and was even willing to give the couple a considerable sum of money. But under one condition: Jules had to become respectable. His father insisted upon buying an interest for him in the office of a stockbroker. In the new Empire there was a lot of money to be made on the stock market, and by being in a firm, Jules would receive a share of the broker's profits.

What could Jules do in his position but accept?

It was very pleasant to move into a nice little apartment in the *Rue Montparnasse*. It was wonderful to honeymoon in England, to see the largest ship of the world, the *Great Eastern*, being built on the Thames, to view the harbor of Liverpool with its tremendous traffic, and finally to make a romantic pilgrimage to the rocky coast of Scotland. But with the return to Paris began a new, dreary, hum-drum life.

From eleven in the morning until late in the afternoon Jules was busy at the stock exchange and occupied with exchange rates and drafts and stocks, which did not interest him in the least.

The former bohemian, romantic poet and theatrical secretary, the man who longed to travel through the entire world and to experience adventure on all continents had now become a stockbroker, and his fellows were worthy businessmen who talked only about money and stocks! Jules Verne was confined to rigid office hours with a dull boss who drove him to despair. Jules did all the work without ever setting eyes on any of the promised profits. He did not even tell his wife how miserable he felt in his new position.

Many of his poor artist friends thought that he had won the Grand Prize — he seemed so prosperous to them. They also congratulated him on being a prospective father. But Jules could only see that instead of conquering Paris with his verses, he had now become a *petit bourgeois* who spent his days in a boring and hated profession. He felt that he had succeeded in nothing, and that he, like a hundred thousand others, had to renounce forever the dream of fame, riches, travel, and an interesting life.

While in this mood, Jules Verne met a man with whom he soon became close friends, whom he admired, and who led exactly the sort of life he would have wished for himself.

Felix Tournachon, who as a journalist had taken the name Felix Nadar, was a person of versatility. He was simultaneously a traveling correspondent, permanent contributor to an important periodical, author of well-known fashionable novels, mordant caricaturist, daring sportsman, and, above all, a famous photographer. Furthermore, Nadar was at home everywhere in Paris, and he knew everybody, from the ministers and bankers to the dancers at the grand opera, from scientists who were members of the Academy to the painters living in cheap studios in the Latin Quarter.

Jules Verne had met Nadar at the Scientific Press Club. From the first, the two men liked each other, and they held endless conversations about modern technology and its progress. On one point in particular they were in whole-hearted agreement; the main characteristic of the modern era — they both recognized — lay in the triumph of science and of the human intellect over rebellious, hostile nature.

Felix Nadar was a man of imagination and ideas, and usually he knew how to realize them. One night he came out with a plan which Jules Verne greeted with the greatest enthusiasm. He wanted to build a huge free-floating balloon, which would greatly surpass any of the historical balloons. With this he would make an airborne voyage across all of Europe. A large hall had already been rented for its construction and financial aid had been promised from several quarters.

From now on Jules Verne was utterly fascinated by his friend's project. He busied himself with hundreds of details regarding the construction and flight of balloons, and he finally became the consulting expert. He began to neglect his office

hours, and even the early morning hours of writing in his attic study became less important to him
than this project. If one were looking for Verne,
one was sure to find him in the great hall where
Nadar's *Gigant* (giant) was already nearing completion. This was a super balloon, which would
carry a two-story cabin up into the air, and whose
gas-filled body would have a circumference of
about thirty feet. It was decided that Jules would
certainly take part in this first epoch-making air
voyage.

At last Jules Verne found life bearable again.
He secretly believed that this sensational flight in
the balloon would mark a radical change in his
boring life. If it were successful, might he not become second flight captain to Nadar? Might he
not eventually fly a balloon of his own? And once
they had succeeded in flying across Europe, would
that not open up the entire air mass to navigation?
And might it not then become possible to visit
every continent in a new manner and discover it
from a bird's eye view? This, at last, was an escape
from the dreary everyday world.

Madame Honorine was not very enthusiastic
about her husband's new interests, and he cau-
tiously did not tell her much about his plans for
the future. But secretly he had already bought
himself a telescope and had had a new English
traveling coat made. It was the year 1862, and the

THE MAKING OF A WRITER   33

trial flight of the *Gigant* was scheduled to take place in the beginning of June.

Now the days just flew by. Jules took charge of the proper distribution of instruments and baggage in the cabin of the balloon, and he even had Nadar photograph him as a future air traveler. But when the last arrangements had been made, there were some turbulent days at the stock exchange, and Jules saw no possibility of getting away from his office. He had been absent often enough.

The news that Nadar had set the time of his trial flight ahead reached Verne by chance a full twelve hours after its launching. Soon afterward a further piece of devastating news reached him. The laboriously constructed but much too heavy technological monster had broken away from its cords and had been ruptured a few minutes later.

Felix Nadar took this accident in stride much more easily than his friend Jules Verne. The entire Paris press expressed sympathy for the failure of the trial flight. Nadar knew how to take advantage of this sympathy and used it to interest new backers in his scheme. Soon he was able to announce that work was progressing on a new *Gigant*.

But what about Jules Verne?

He had disappeared from the world, and he no longer appeared in the great hall where work on a new cabin was progressing. He had notified his office that he was sick. He had already spent several days brooding in his attic study, and Madame Honorine was obliged to carry up meals, which he barely touched.

This had indeed been enough to drive him to despair. For months, he had lived on the hope of adventure that he had placed in the trial flight of the *Gigant*. Once again he had fallen from his dreams into a reality, which seemed more hopeless now than ever before.

It might take a year or even longer until Nadar would be ready for the next flight, and Jules could not wait that long. In order to escape from his depression, Jules Verne again turned, as he had done so many times before, to the realm of fantasy. He began to scribble on a piece of paper. It was the beginning of a logbook, written aboard the cabin of a balloon. He saw himself and Nadar floating above northern France! Then his disappointment welled up once more and made him stop.

On his desk lay a half-finished manuscript, a report about recent explorations in Africa. He should have finished it long ago and ought to have sent it off to the publisher. Public interest in the "dark continent" had mounted in the last few years. Only recently the Englishmen Richard F. Burton and John H. Speke had attempted to advance to the mysterious sources of the Nile, and had discovered the huge Lake Victoria instead.

David Livingstone, whose first sensational travels in South Africa and whose discovery of the Zambezi River had earned him considerable fame, was now on his second great expedition into the African interior and his return was awaited with suspense.

Half unwillingly, Jules Verne began to look through all his notes for the report on Africa. Suddenly it struck him that it would be a thrilling adventure to explore Africa from a balloon — to *fly* over the mountains and waterfalls that stand in the way of a land expedition and to see darkest Africa spread out below as on a map! How thrilling to be in a balloon above the dark continent and head for the Zambezi River or Lake Victoria, to look down on the jungle near Lake Nyasa where Livingstone had disappeared, to discover secret Arab slave markets in the interior, and native villages with their exotic tribes, previously known only by hearsay! A journey by balloon over Africa — Africa with its magnificent landscapes, its steppes, rivers, waterfalls, jungles, and volcanoes! Would a report like that not be much more fascinating than the one he had begun to write?

It would have to be a balloon that could be steered and whose supply of gases could be replenished again and again. Feverishly, Jules Verne began to make sketches and calculations and to set up a route for the journey.

And then he began to write. He wrote in the mornings from six until noon, and again from the early afternoon until after nightfall. He had forgotten Nadar and even himself; unwittingly he had become transformed into a certain Dr. Ferguson, a rich and adventurous gentleman. This gentleman had built a balloon and had found a traveling companion; now he appears before the world-famous Royal Geographical Society in London to submit his completely new and unheard-of project. . . .

Thus begins the first chapter of the fantastic and unreal logbook, with which Jules Verne consoled himself for his disappointments. Madame Honorine must have thought that her husband had received an especially important commission from an important periodical, for she always found him working at his desk. Instead of going to his office and fulfilling his everyday duties like any ordinary man, Jules Verne, the stockbroker, was gliding over Africa for days and weeks on the wings of his imagination.

Jules Verne's Dr. Ferguson and his companion encountered the most incredible adventures almost every hour. Their balloon, whose trial rope dangled above the crowns of gigantic jungle trees, had been christened *Victoria*. There were enough foodstuffs on board, and an ingeniously constructed apparatus made it possible to replenish the gases that escaped from the balloon's covering, so that the trip could be prolonged beyond any span previously believed possible.

The *Victoria* appeared in the teeming markets of deepest Africa, and was adored by the natives as a foreign god. She remained moored on the crown of a tremendous breadfruit tree in order to be safe from attack, and in the evening she landed noiselessly in the tall grass close to a native village where a great ceremonial dance was just in progress. She narrowly escaped the most harrowing dangers.

Once, during a low flight, the trail rope became entangled in the tusks of an elephant who, half-crazed with fright, began to race over the grass-steppes with the *Victoria* in tow. Only in the moment of final distress was the balloon saved by a well-aimed shot. The *Victoria* traveled across the equator and approached gurgling waterfalls; she carried her small crew over the sources of the Nile, hitherto not seen by any human eye; and she escaped from the center of a terrible tropical storm by rising high above the clouds and the flashes of lightning.

Whatever Jules Verne knew about Africa, meteorology, geography, and about balloons and aviation found its way effortlessly into the manuscript; and after a while he suddenly realized that he had never before written with such ease. Ideas came swarming, and in his haste he could hardly put them on paper in the form of short notes.

The longer the journey went on, the greater became the technical difficulties of the trip. But again and again they were solved in the last moment in a convincing fashion, until finally every last shred of ballast had to be thrown overboard, and nothing could be saved except the bare lives of the travelers. Without the cabin, merely hanging on to the net of the sinking balloon, the crew of the *Victoria* travels across the entire width of the foaming Senegal River, thereby making a last minute escape! This is the culminating moment of a breathtaking air journey of almost five weeks' duration.

Jules Verne awakened from his dream only when he had written the word "End" at the bottom of his manuscript.

3 THE FIRST NOVEL OF THE FUTURE

WHEN JULES VERNE emerged once again from his attic, he had succeeded in writing his disappointment out of his system. He first paid a visit to Nadar, who was already working on the plans for a new *Gigant*. Then he went to his office, and after an unusually angry discussion with his partner, he returned home in a rather dejected mood. Only then did he confess to his wife what he had been up to during the last four weeks. Madame Honorine asked him to show her the manuscript. To her husband's great surprise she found the manuscript, *Five Weeks in a Balloon*, fascinating. She thought that a Parisian publisher might be interested in it and encouraged him to send his manuscript to the editors of an important newspaper.

He sent the manuscript off four times, and each time it was returned to him. The criticism was always more or less the same: the story dealt too much with science and technology. There was no exciting murder contained in it or even a "great passion" for a beautiful woman to spice it up a bit. Certainly the author could not expect an editor to offer *this* to readers! Thus one of France's greatest authors began his career by having a manuscript returned by all the editors he contacted with polite refusals.

But Madame Honorine would not let Jules give up so easily, and he agreed to make one final attempt, after his friend Nadar had suggested one more prospect.

At number 18 *Rue Jacob,* a street on Paris' Left Bank, famous for its booksellers and publishers, Jules Hetzel had established his office, which specialized in books for young people. He was planning to issue a periodical that would be of interest to young people and their families, and was looking for a good writer who would help him launch his new magazine.

Jules Verne was persuaded to send his manuscript to Hetzel. A week went by, ten days, and finally two weeks had passed and there was still no reply. After a fortnight, Jules Verne lost his patience; he appeared at the office in the *Rue Jacob* at noon and asked to speak to Hetzel.

A quarter of an hour later he was shown in, and

found himself in a bedroom for Hetzel was accustomed to spending his mornings in bed. The publisher himself was in his dressing gown, eating breakfast at a small table, with the manuscript lying beside him.

Hetzel was an undersized little man with intelligent eyes and a deeply furrowed face; he had experienced much grief in his lifetime, and had been forced to leave Paris for a long period for political reasons.

"I am very sorry, Mr. Verne," Hetzel began. "Your work has great merit, but. . . ."

"Thank you, that's all I wanted to know," Jules Verne replied angrily. "Just give it back to me, and I won't trouble you any longer."

Hetzel regarded his visitor and shook his head in amazement.

"And what else do you do besides writing, Mr. Verne?"

"If you want to know, I'm at the Exchange. The commodities in which I. . . ."

"Do you make much money at it?" the publisher interrupted him.

"At the Exchange? Not at all. I am not interested in that profession. I. . . ."

Hetzel interrupted him again. "Then give up that nonsense altogether, and come write for me."

"But . . . I thought you didn't want my manuscript?"

"This manuscript? It is much too short for me.

It is not written with enough attention to detail. I want the characters delineated more carefully.

"The sequence of adventures must be changed, and you have to make the entire story about twice as long."

"I am sorry, I cannot do that," Jules Verne replied stubbornly. "I have enjoyed writing it, the manuscript is finished, and I won't alter a single line. I'll just take it back, if you please."

Once more the publisher stared at him. Then he took off his gold-rimmed glasses and asked: "I guess you don't know what you have done here? I can see that you have no idea. You have what it takes to be a great author! I want you to make a good novel out of this for me. Do you think that you could write other travel stories like this?"

Now it was Jules Verne's turn to be completely baffled.

"I could turn one out every month easily, Mr. Hetzel. I have read enough about travels. We could have a long journey by steamer. . . ."

"That's fine," the publisher interrupted him for the third time. "I don't want a story from you every month, just two each year. Here, take your manuscript and expand it in the way I have indicated. If you accept my offer, I will give you a contract which will permit you to give up your present occupation."

"Pardon me, but what more or less would this contract entail?"

The reply came as such a surprise to Jules Verne, that he first thought that he had not heard right.

"I will pay you 20,000 gold *francs* for two stories each year. But first I want this manuscript changed. There are not enough ideas in it yet. Come back in four weeks, and right now go and get an advance of 2,000 *francs* from the accountant. Good-bye, Mr. Verne."

"Not enough ideas . . . !" The shrewd Hetzel knew how to deal with people, and particularly with authors. He knew that this remark would spur Verne on. And the young author went home muttering under his breath, in spite of the 2,000 *francs* in his pocket. But in his study, as he read through the manuscript once again, it was as though he suddenly saw it through different eyes. There was much that needed to be rewritten, and some parts were actually only the bare outlines of exciting episodes.

Even during this first rereading of his manuscript several great new adventures came to Jules' mind. He now remembered what Alexandre Dumas had taught him during those early days. He reworked the entire plot and conceived a third character in the person of Dr. Ferguson's clever and humorous valet. The plot moved more swiftly and the suspense became intensified. Exactly four weeks later he returned his completed manuscript to Hetzel.

In the ensuing months, Jules Vernes was to learn what a remarkable person his publisher was. Hetzel went through the manuscript with him line for line, striking out every inconsistency and improbability and pointing out the weak spots. During these sessions, which took place in Hetzel's office, usually in the evening after business hours, Jules Verne discovered his own peculiar way of writing; in fact, he discovered himself, the author Jules Verne.

"Let me know your new plans soon," Hetzel had encouraged him. "You shall write a whole series of 'extraordinary journeys' for me. You will see, readers will respond with enthusiasm if we offer them something completely new and different! You know quite a lot about the sciences; all this must go into the new stories."

"Mr. Hetzel, do you really think that my manuscript will be a success?"

"Don't worry, you won't have any cause for complaint," Hetzel replied dryly.

On New Year's Day 1863, the Parisians who strolled past the bookstore displays discovered that a novel with a most unusual title had been published by Hetzel: *Five Weeks in a Balloon.*

This title became the talk of the town. During

the next few days passersby thronged into the book stores on the *Boulevard Saint-Germain*. The displays of books were hidden by a sea of top hats and crinoline bonnets; and before the week was over, the first edition of the book was already sold out.

Five weeks in a balloon? Until then, any balloon journey had lasted only a few hours and covered very short distances. Some people assumed that the balloon in Verne's book was the same one in which the famous Felix Nadar had tried to take off. Thanks to this misunderstanding, the second edition was sold out after a month. Soon it was followed by a third, fourth, and fifth edition. Everybody talked about this novel and about its hitherto completely unknown author, Jules Verne.

Jules Verne had given his readers something they had been waiting for, something completely new, in subject matter as well as style. The public hailed this mad journey over Africa in a balloon as much more interesting, exciting, and above all, much more timely than all the high-society romanticism of other current novels.

Verne's book made its readers, who soon numbered in the hundred thousands, realize clearly that the age of technology and modern science had begun and that they were already in the midst of a new era which promised many new and fascinating marvels. The earth, the seas, and the

sky would all be conquered now in an entirely
new way. And all this would happen within their
lifetime!

At the same time, Jules Verne presented his
readers with a new kind of hero, who was not a
*marqui*s of the eighteenth century but a contemporary man, a hero not unlike the thousands of
engineers, inventors, and scientists who were already hard at work shaping a new technological
civilization. Cool and self-reliant, Dr. Ferguson
had the ability to plan on a large scale and calculate with precision. He was a man of iron energy
who could systematically carry out his plans and
was never at a loss for a solution to his problems.
Yet, he was also a man with a heart and real
feeling for the wonders of nature — this was indeed
a *modern* hero.

Another thing which enthralled Jules Verne's
readers was the breathtaking speed with which he
unfolded his adventures. There was no need here
to wade through long, dull descriptions and endless dialogue of the sort usually found in fashionable novels. One adventure swiftly followed the
other, but one never knew in advance what the
outcome would be; almost every second page held
another surprise. Modern science fiction had been
born.

German and English translations appeared simultaneously with the second French edition. In

Paris, Berlin, London, and New York, boys pretended that they were balloonists, and even among their elders taking a balloon trip became the fashionable thing to do. The fad finally reached such tremendous proportions that the publisher of an American newspaper organized balloon races. Later, he even sent his best reporter to explore the interior of Africa. This reporter, Henry Morton Stanley, had adventures that read like something out of a Jules Verne story, and eventually became world-famous as the explorer of the Congo River.

For the time being, however, reality was somewhat less spectacular than the audacious inventions of Verne's book. Early in October 1863, some ten thousand Parisians gathered at the *Champ de Mars* to witness the first journey of Nadar's new *Gigant*, which had finally been completed. They admired the huge gas-filled sphere and the two-story cabin.

Only Jules Verne was not among the spectators. He was already at work on a new book, and his publisher was urging him to finish the manuscript as quickly as possible, since he had signed a contract to do ten books in five years — at 20,000 gold francs a year.

As for Felix Nadar's balloon, after an unfortunate failure to take off at all, it finally rose and traveled due east until it crossed the Rhine. It was forced to come down before reaching Hanover, however, in a dangerous crash landing that almost killed Nadar and his wife. This flight received so much sensational publicity in the newspapers—for in spite of the accident the *Gigant* had achieved a significant advance in aerial flight—that Jules Verne's book gained thousands of new readers. But would the young author really have enough power of invention to find enough material to fulfill his contract?

"What will you write for me next?" Hetzel asked him anxiously.

"It will be something completely new and different, Mr. Hetzel," replied Jules Verne, and he paused for a moment to heighten the suspense. "This time it will be a trip through the universe — to the moon."

Hetzel was completely dumbfounded and amazed.

"To the moon? But won't that appear too improbable to the reader?"

"Not at all," Verne replied. "The trip will be prepared in accordance with the very latest scientific discoveries. I can already reveal to you that it will take exactly ninety-seven hours and twenty minutes."

"Well I'll be darned! If you succeed. . . ." Hetzel exclaimed delightedly.

A trip to the moon in the year 1863! Only now,

over a hundred years later, is Jules Verne's "dream" about to be realized.

In January 1863, people who had been waiting impatiently for a new novel by Jules Verne were taken aback when they saw this improbable book title: *Journey from the Earth to the Moon,* direct passage in 97 hours and 20 minutes.

Soon the new book had found its way into many fashionable drawing rooms, into the small lending libraries, and was even to be found on the night table of the Empress Eugénie. Scientists and scholars, who had started to read the story with amusement, soon were amazed by the extremely accurate calculations on which Verne's moon flight was based. To an even greater extent than *Five Weeks in a Balloon,* this book opened up a completely new realm.

Today, when we read this astonishing "best-seller" of 1863, we are still captivated and amazed. Now we can fully appreciate the genius of Jules Verne and his uncanny predictions of the future. *Journey from the Earth to the Moon* is actually — though dressed in the costume of the period — the very first believable novel of the future ever written, and the experiences that Jules Verne described so vividly in it *still* lie ahead of us.

Let us see how Jules envisioned the future in this book, which he set in the United States. The book begins with an amazing announcement: At a meeting of the Baltimore Gun Club the president of the club submits a fabulous plan to his fellow members — he intends to shoot at the moon with a super-cannon. The famous Cambridge Observatory is asked for a detailed opinion about such a project, and the scientists consider it theoretically quite possible that a projectile could reach the moon under certain conditions.

Five and a half million dollars have been collected from many nations, and the construction of the *Columbiad* can begin. But where! A search is started for a launching site in a remote area. Although Texas competed ardently for this honor, a site is finally chosen on the Florida peninsula. And this is where today, at Cape Kennedy, we find launching pads for space missiles! The launching is to take place on December 1, because on that day the position of the full moon is closest to the earth.

Meanwhile, a world-famous French scientist, Michel Ardan, is on his way to the United States. He proves to the Gun Club and to the public that the new moon-projectile should not be round like a cannon ball, but elongated like a rocket!

Then Ardan announces that he intends to be a passenger on the moon trip! Public enthusiasm knows no bounds. Impey Barbicane, the president of the Gun Club, and his adversary, Captain Nicholl, who has placed several bets against the successful outcome of the venture, have no other alternative but to join the daring, witty, and always-cheerful Frenchman.

The missile's interior is built for comfortable travel. The cabin is furnished in the lavish style of the period, and at last, everything is ready. But shouldn't there first be a test to determine how living beings react at such great altitudes, and whether they are able to survive beyond the atmosphere around the earth? Of course!

Jules Verne thought of this, too — a hundred years before our time! A test flight is launched with a tomcat and a squirrel as passengers. The missile returns to earth and falls into the ocean. Ships are standing by and divers retrieve the capsule. The hatch is opened, and the tomcat jumps out, hale and hearty. He has even had a meal on his journey — his former companion, the squirrel!

In the meantime, a huge telescope has been completed. Now the journey to the moon can be followed from the earth. Jules Verne's imaginary telescope is installed on a peak in the great Rocky Mountains not far from San Francisco. Today, the Hale Telescope, the world's largest, stands on Mount Palomar close to the site Jules Verne chose.

"Thanks to its tremendous optical power the depths of the heavens could be explored to the utmost limits," writes Jules Verne about *his* telescope. Since 1949 it *has* been possible to photograph, with the aid of the Hale Telescope, the heights of the universe and stars that are a billion light-years from earth.

The day of the launching arrives. Five million spectators have flocked to Florida and have appeared near the launching area. Many of them are living in a tent city.

The glistening, silver-colored projectile is lowered into the shaft of the cannon. Now the crowds begin to cheer as the three daredevil moon travelers appear on the launching field. Between the two Americans we catch sight of Michel Ardan, puffing on a cigar. He is accompanied by a hound and a huge Newfoundland dog. He appears to be as cheerful and untroubled as Jules Verne's friend Felix Nadar was when the *Gigant* was launched. Actually, the name Ardan is an anagram of the name NADAR.

The three men climb into the interior of the missile. The hatch is screwed shut, the derricks and scaffolding are removed from the scene. Gradually, a hush settles over the crowd in the launching area in expectation of the take-off. Meanwhile, the three men settle down in the interior of their well-padded missile.

They find themselves in an elegant little gaslit drawing room. Food supplies for a whole year have been stowed away in the missile, as well as moon maps, hunting rifles, and — last but not least — Michel Ardan's cigars.

After checking the time by their watches, the three men stretch out on thick mattresses in order to withstand the tremendous impact of the take-off, just as missile pilots do today.

It is now 10:46, and only forty seconds remain before take-off! At the launching pad the count-down begins, exactly as it is now done at Cape Kennedy, except that instead of counting backward to zero, as we do today, here the count goes up . . . 38, 39, and 40 seconds.

And here is the scene as Jules Verne wrote it:

Fire!
In that instant Murchison pressed the button of the ignition device, thereby establishing the current and hurling an electric spark into the depths of the cannon. A terrible, thunderlike detonation ensued, the likes of which had never been heard before, with such roaring and flashing that it exceeded anything imaginable. A huge column of fire shot out from the ground as from a crater. The earth trembled; some of the spectators momentarily caught sight of the projectile, as it triumphantly shot through fiery vapors up into the atmosphere. The streak of white-hot flame which rose to the heavens spread its light over all of Florida. . . .

The space missile — a hundred years ago!
The missile hurtles into space. The spectators

gradually regain their senses after the deafening
roar and the atmospheric pressure caused by the
rocket, which threw even the ships in the harbor
into confusion. Now everybody tries, with telescopes and field glasses, to discover the projectile
in the sky.

And here Jules Verne surprises us with one of
those unexpected ideas, which had gained for the
gifted storyteller such a huge number of admirers.
For just at this point, when we would give anything to know what has happened to the missile,
and whether it is really on its way to the moon,
the clear sky suddenly clouds over.

To the despair of the spectators, the moon
remains invisible for ten long days. Unless there is
a break in the clouds very soon, it is unlikely that
the projectile can still be seen, for on December
11 the moon will go into its fourth phase. But on
the eleventh day, the sky is finally swept clear by
an east wind, and through the new gigantic telescope people on earth are able to detect, in the
vicinity of the moon, a tiny black dot.

But in the meantime something completely un-
foreseen has taken place. The Cambridge Observatory gives its scientific opinion about this new
development. For, contrary to all calculations, the
missile has not reached its goal, but has only at-
tained the orbit of the moon, and it is now circling
the moon as a new star, a satellite! Perhaps one

day the gravity of the moon will predominate, allowing the travelers to make a landing. Otherwise, writes the director of the Cambridge Astronomical Observatory, the projectile shall continue to circle around the moon in an unchanging orbit until the end of the world.

What has happened? How do the travelers in the missile feel about all this? Are they still alive?

In order to find out the answers to all these questions readers of the novel had to purchase a second volume. Jules Verne's publisher knew his business. The first part of the story ends with an announcement by the secretary of the Gun Club, who had followed the path of the rocket through the huge telescope.

"We shall have news from them and they shall hear from us," he tells the newspapermen who besiege him about the travelers in the missile. "They are intelligent and inventive men who have all the aids of science at their disposal. With these, it is possible to achieve whatever one will, and we shall soon see how they extricate themselves from their predicament."

The first part of the journey to the moon appeared serially in one of the largest Parisian newspapers, the *Journal des Debats*. Immediately, the number of subscribers rose and impatient readers demanded the publication of the complete book. A few days after its publication, the first edition

was already out of print. Several editions of the
second volume were prepared and distributed in
advance, and translations into English and German
appeared almost simultaneously.

The second volume, *Round Moon*, the story
of the actual journey around the moon, was told
in such swift, bold strokes and with so much of
Verne's usual humor and charm that the reader
learned all that was known at the time about the
neighboring planets, conditions in outer space, and
in addition, was treated to some bold prophecies
and theories which began to attract the notice of
scientists.

Would it really be like this, when someday —
the idea was almost unthinkable — man would fly
to the moon? Today we still ask many of the
same questions that Verne's readers asked in 1863.
And he answered some questions that very few
people, even scientists, were asking in those days.

For example, the three scientists in the missile
ask one another why they had not heard any
sound, any kind of explosion, at the take-off. Jules
Verne supplies them with the answer to this rid-
dle: the missile is flying faster than the speed of
sound — an amazing and, for the general public of
that day, a most sensational deduction!

An unbearable heat radiates from the walls, the
thermometer reads 45 degrees centigrade. The
heat it generated by friction in the atmosphere —

a factor which even today is one of the greatest
problems encountered in leaving and re-entering
the earth's atmosphere. But Michel Ardan reas-
sures his two companions; they will shortly reach
outer space, and then it will get much colder.

The cabin has four tightly locked portholes for
looking out, one of them directly under their
feet. Now they remove the metal sheets. Outside
there is nothing but the blackest darkness — the
darkness of the universe, lit only by a few stars.

Soon moonlight shines into the missile's interior so that the gas lamps are no longer needed.
The description of the view of the earth from
space is so vivid that it is like seeing it on a movie
screen. Along with the three travelers we look
down to observe the mountains that stand out
against the earth. Soon a ring of clouds hides
these from view. What we see here reminds us
exactly of the photographs of the earth's surface,
made from space by the automatic cameras which
we have at our disposal today.

Journey from the Earth to the Moon is still
published as the classic novel of the future, and
we find countless editions of it all over the world.
In this second volume we find descriptions of the
sensation of intoxication at high altitudes, which
has long since been observed scientifically in test
cabins. We read of retro-rockets, which play such
an important part in space flights today. There is

only one big difference between Jules Verne's
moon journey of 1863 and the moon journey that
will probably soon become an actuality. Verne's
three characters travel in comfort and ease, without foregoing any of the conveniences. They travel
through space just as though they were stitting in
a pleasant drawing room in Paris, a feature which
we encounter again in many of Jules Verne's
adventures.

His characters are not dressed like monsters of
technology in fantastic space suits, helmets, and
oxygen masks. They travel in everyday clothes.
They eat ordinary food. Michel Ardan sees to it
that they are served a good breakfast and an
even more delicious dinner every day. They drink
wine and smoke cigars.

They travel through the air in a drawing room,
just as in another Verne novel, Professor Pierre
Arronax and his companions will travel through
the depths of the ocean in an even more sumptuous
salon.

Yet even though these luxurious quarters seem
quaint to us today, they served a purpose in
Verne's novels. Jules Verne's readers, sitting in
their own drawing rooms, felt they were sharing
in the experience of space travel. It was as if they
had only to look out of their own windows to
see the meteors passing by and the huge disk of
the moon coming closer.

From their armchairs, Verne's readers received a detailed "guided tour" of the moon from very close up. The fascination of Verne's description lies entirely in the *factual* information we are given about the moon! Unlike so many pseudo-scientific novels, Jules Verne does not need to resort to moon people or similar nonsense. He describes only what had actually been observed — but only with the help of telescopes. These "facts" proved more overwhelming than the fantasies of other writers.

The climax to Verne's novel *Journey from the Earth to the Moon* is reached as the distance between the missile and the moon becomes greater. Already the surface of the moon appears distant and hazy. Soon the space travelers will reach the decisive point where, according to their careful calculations, the gravity of the moon will either be great enough to pull them toward it until they plunge on to its surface, or they will fall back to earth.

They now do their utmost to reach the moon; they shoot off their retro-rockets in the hope that this will propel them on to the moon. The projectile moves toward the moon, followed by a fiery trail, but the force is not great enough. They crowd against the window and notice that the moon is very rapidly moving away from them. They are falling, hurtling back through space toward earth. They land in the Pacific Ocean and are recovered in much the same way as today's astronauts.

Jules Verne's heroes blazed the way to the stars. At the book's end, a society to map traffic routes through the stars is founded. The traffic director: Michel Ardan.

"One day," Verne says in this book, "we shall travel to the planets and stars just as today we take a trip to Liverpool or to New York, with ease, speed, and safety through the ocean of air."

This was Jules Verne's prophecy in his book, a truly unthinkable prospect in the year 1863!

But it awakened the enthusiasm of millions, and drew the attention of thousands of engineers and technicians to a field which today, a hundred years later, has long since left the realm of makebelieve.

A NEW CELEBRITY

In the spring of 1864 about "five hundred persons of the male sex," most of them young, called at the offices of the publisher Hetzel and at Jules Verne's home on the *Rue Montparnasse*. They wanted to join Jules Verne on a trip to the moon and had come to apply in advance! Naturally both Hetzel and Jules Verne were delighted by these visits, but Madame Honorine was dismayed by the constant stream of visitors.

Even in our time, hundreds of Americans and thousands of young Russians have already put in their bid for the first trip to the moon. In the United States, travel bureaus have even been asked if they have tickets to sell for the first tourist flight to the moon.

61

Although the author of *Journey from the Earth to the Moon* received each of the aspiring moon travelers and chatted with him, he actually had no time at all for such visitors. His contract with Hetzel made it urgent for him to complete a third novel in short order.

Verne's new book was to appear serially in Hetzel's magazine for young people, and the mere fact that Jules Verne was to be the author assured the success of the venture in advance and gained an unusual number of subscribers for the magazine. This was the third "extraordinary journey" to be experienced by Jules Verne's readers, and again it would be a book in which he the author was to "invent" a bit of the future.

Hetzel had kept the title of the new novel a secret until the first serial appeared in the magazine. From then on almost everyone in France, both young and old, waited in suspense for each new installment of *The Adventures of Captain Hatteras.*

The author left his readers completely in the dark as to the kind of adventure Captain Hatteras would have. As a matter of fact, the Captain did not even appear in the first few installments. The novel begins with this news item in a Liverpool newspaper:

"Tomorrow, at low tide, the brig 'Forward' will go to sea from the New Princess Docks. Destination unknown!"

A most unusual ship, this *Forward*.

She had already attracted the attention of sea captains and sailors in the harbor of Liverpool because of her strange shape. She was broad and heavy like the whaling boats that ply the waters of the Far North and must withstand the pressure of ice packs. But she was even sturdier than a whale boat. On her bow the *Forward* carried a sharp blade of cast steel — presumably for hacking through ice. Would her destination be the Arctic Ocean, one of the most dangerous areas of navigation? Or would she possibly be heading for the North Pole, which had never been approached?

The departure of the *Forward* was very secretive. Nobody, not even the crew, knew who had ordered this strange ship to be built, or who was in command of her. Officers of the crew had received mysterious letters signed only: "Captain of the *Forward*." Only bachelors had been accepted as crewmen, and each one was paid five times the usual wage, and received five hundred pounds cash in advance. The officers were paid even more handsomely.

Finally, the mysterious ship departs without her captain on board. Only during the northward journey, as the *Forward* fights her way through murderous icebergs, does Captain Hatteras finally appear.

He tells his frightened crew that their destination is the North Pole. In the year 1864 the conquest of the North Pole was considered an utter impossibility. Too many daring attempts had foundered in the eternal ice. Willem Barents had made the first attempt in 1596 and failed. All the great explorers who came after him, Vitus Bering, Captain James Cook, John Ross, and finally Sir John Franklin, had foundered.

Franklin had set out for the North Pole on May 19, 1845. He and his crew of 134 men had never returned. Franklin and all those who had taken part in the expedition were officially declared dead by the English government in 1854, but Franklin's widow continued to spend her fortune financing new search parties.

In 1858, six years before the publication of *Captain Hatteras*, the English Sir Francis Leopold MacClintock finally succeeded, with the help of Eskimos, in discovering Franklin's trail. In the eternal snows of the far North, he found notebooks and documents that had belonged to the Franklin expedition. The final find was a sled surrounded by skeletons.

World interest in polar expeditions was at such a pitch in 1864 that any novel about the North Pole was assured of a world-wide audience. Such a novel by Jules Verne could not fail, particularly since he was a real authority on the subject. For years, Verne had been reading and collecting every scrap of information that he could find on the land of "eternal ice."

Once more Verne opened up a completely new world to his readers. From the pages of Verne's new novel they learned about the dangers of this glacial wasteland with its menacing ice drifts. Even sea captains and geographers took this "novel for young people" seriously.

The plot of the novel is full of suspense. When the *Forward* becomes stuck in the ice, Captain Hatteras and his men leave their ship in order to attempt to reach the Pole by sled. This is just what Franklin had done. It is then that Captain Hatteras learns that he has competition in his venture. An American crew has also set out for the Pole by sled. But most of the Americans perish; only their leader escapes death. Now the Englishmen and the American captain forge ahead together, finally reaching the Pole after many hardships.

But, at the moment of victory, Captain Hatteras is no longer in his right mind. The strain of the trek has deranged his intellect.

The end of the novel is truly unforgettable. The sick Captain Hatteras is brought to a sanatorium near Liverpool:

For some time now Hatteras was wont to take long walks every day in the company of his faithful dog, who always regarded him with sad and gentle eyes. But these walks were always and invariably made in one and the same direction, they always went along a certain path leading up from Sten Cottage. Whenever the Captain had reached the end of the path, he would return by walking backwards. If anyone stopped him, he would point with his fingers to a certain point in the sky.

Whenever someone would try to induce him to turn around he would become angry, and the dog Tell, who shared his master's wrath, would bark furiously.

The doctor carefully observed this strange mania and soon understood the reason for this stubborn peculiarity. He was able to guess why Hatteras would always walk in the same direction, as though under the influence of some magnetic force.

Captain Hatteras was forever marching due North!

Millions of readers all over the world began to take a lively interest in the exploration of the North Pole. The conquest of the North Pole became an enticing goal. Wealthy patrons made large sums available for the exploration of the Arctic Ocean.

And the experts, seamen as well as scientists, began to discuss the exciting details of Captain

Hatteras' preparations for his journey. They marveled that Verne sitting at his desk in Paris could write so convincingly and in such minute detail of the preparations needed to insure the success of a polar expedition. We mention here only one detail of these preparations, which was later adopted by every polar expedition in almost exactly the same form—namely the polar diet. Jules Verne equipped his explorers with vitamins, which were almost unheard of in those days. Verne considered vitamins far more important food for an Arctic expedition than chocolate or preserved meats.

Verne also had barrels of lemon juice, mashed sorrel, and calcium tablets loaded for the voyage of the *Forward*. These three items were proven preventatives for scurvy, the seamen's dread disease.

The nutritional mainstay which Verne suggested was pemmican, known for many centuries as the "iron rations" of the North American Indian. Pemmican is a combination of beef that had been dried in the sun mixed with pulverized suet, or fat.

Once a polar expedition had left its ship and begun the march across the ice with sleds, it became necessary again and again to find new ways to combat the vicissitudes of nature. Verne drew on the experience of the Eskimos. When an icy blizzard made it impossible to pitch tents, he had Captain Hatteras' men hurriedly build an igloo.

Such details, taken from the wealth of material that Jules Verne had collected in his scientific notes, come alive in his book. The influence of this accurately documented book was to be far-reaching. It inspired a few of its young readers to consider the conquest of the North Pole as their life's work. Decades later these young readers — Fridtjof Nansen, Salomon Andree, Roald Amundsen, Robert F. Scott, and Admiral Richard Byrd — would indeed explore the Arctic regions and finally discover the Pole.

The race to reach the Pole that Verne described would actually take place forty-seven years later at the South Pole instead of the North. The two men involved were Robert F. Scott, an Englishman, and Roald Amundsen, a Norwegian. During his own lifetime, Jules Verne was able to follow with interest a number of adventurous polar expeditions, which were all a preparation for the final conquest of the North Pole.

In 1879, the famous American newspaper publisher, Gordon Bennett, fitted out the "Jeanette Expedition" at a tremendous cost. All hands perished in the eternal ice of the Arctic polar region.

In 1893, the young Norwegian, Fridtjof Nansen, started out for the North Pole. He christened his ship "Fram" which means "Forward," after Captain Hatteras' ship.

The *Fram* was a combination steamer and sailing vessel, just like her namesake in the novel. With this ship, Nansen traveled upon the famous polar drift, leaving it when he had reached the closest point to the pole, in order to continue his journey by sled. He came closer to reaching the North Pole than any man before him.

But one particular polar journey seemed to be conceived utterly in the spirit of Jules Verne. This was Salomon Andree's balloon expedition to the pole. Andree, a Swedish engineer, was a great admirer of Jules Verne. He believed that he could conquer the Pole in a balloon! The scientists rejected his plan categorically. At one of the lectures he gave in order to raise funds for his projected flight, a professor of geography shouted to Andree: "You ought to be writing novels like Jules Verne."

But the public greeted Andree's plan with great enthusiasm, perhaps because it was so much like Dr. Ferguson's balloon journey over Africa. When the first balloon failed, people contributed huge sums of money so that a second flight could be undertaken. We are reminded of the subscription lists which served to finance Dr. Ferguson in Jules Verne's *Journey Over Africa*.

Just like Dr. Ferguson, Andree had to invent some device that would make it possible for him to steer his balloon. He finally rigged up sails.

By adjusting the sails according to the direction of the wind, he hoped to be able to avoid unfavorable air currents.

The *Eagle* started out on July 11, 1897, from the Danish Isles off Spitsbergen. From the outset of the journey it seemed as if reality were imitating one of Jules Verne's novels.

The newspapers of the entire world were following Andree's daring adventure minute by minute. Immediately after take-off, the wind pressed the balloon down so close to the rough sea that the cabin was dunked into the foamy waves. In order to surface, Andree was forced to jettison much of his needed ballast. When the balloon was finally airborne again, it disappeared toward the north.

A message brought by a carrier pigeon and a letter in a bottle, which had been dropped into the sea, were all that was heard from the expedition — after these, silence.

Andree's destiny remained a mystery until twelve years after the end of World War I. In August 1930, a seal hunter found a boat hook on a small island in the Arctic Ocean. This chance find led him to all that remained of Andree's brave expedition. He found several human skeletons and a special treasure — Andree's diaries. From these it was learned that the balloon had only flown for three days before it had become completely frozen. The crew had made a forced landing in the icebound Arctic region. Like Captain Hatteras, Andree and his men set out on sleds over the ice drifts in search of the Pole. Their death march lasted eighty-three days, finally leading them to White Island, where one by one they succumbed to utter exhaustion.

On April 16, 1909, Robert E. Peary, an American, finally made it and raised his country's flag on the North Pole. But Jules Verne was no longer alive to witness another of his prophecies come true.

It was this novel about the discovery of the North Pole which really established Jules Verne's fame as the first author to write a type of believable fiction that was based on sound scientific research. This was science fiction of the highest order. His *Journey from the Earth to the Moon* was also "scientific" but it had been so far ahead of even the wildest dreams of his contemporaries that few thought of it in terms of actual reality.

The discovery of the North Pole was a completely different matter. Here Verne had dealt with a problem which had long since challenged man's imagination and ingenuity. The careful and extremely accurate preparation of this book, and the ingenious way in which the author had seized on the very factors which later on were to prove of the utmost importance in polar expeditions, gave this book its very special importance over and beyond its value as a well-told story.

Above all, Jules Verne had achieved something only accomplished by the greatest writers — in the figure of Captain Hatteras he had created a character that inspired others to heroic efforts in order that they might follow in his footsteps.

Upon completion of the manuscript *The Adventures of Captain Hatteras*, Madame Honorine firmly demanded that her husband stop writing for a while. Day after day had been spent either in his study or in the libraries, and his family (which now included a small son, Michel Verne, as well as Madame Honorine's two daughters) had seen him only at mealtime. Furthermore, the Vernes' pressing financial worries were over, and Madame Honorine now wanted to enjoy life a little. She wanted to stroll through Paris with her husband and to go with him to the opera and the theater. She wanted to entertain, and above all, she wished for a new apartment. Surely, she felt they could at last give up the modest flat in the *Rue Montparnasse*.

Hetzel was also of the opinion that, after three successful books, his author had earned a vacation. On the other hand, he was businessman enough to realize that the world was waiting for Jules Verne's next novel, and he felt that Verne should take advantage of his public's enthusiasm immediately. As usual, Hetzel worried about the subject of his author's new book. Would Verne once more have an extraordinary and original idea? Hetzel's worries were soon dispelled. Jules Verne had found his element as a writer. His new idea proved to be equally as stupendous as any of his others!

The inspiration for his new topic had come to him on one of those dreary winter afternoons when he had found refuge in the Paris libraries. It was a subject that had a mysterious attraction for him, and one which had been fraught with mystery since earliest times. Verne planned to write about the great caves that lay beneath the earth's surface, and that had defied exploration.

Where did these caves lead? To what depths did they reach? Would it perhaps be possible to reach the fiery heart of a volcano through them? Interest in this fascinating subject reached a new high when Hetzel's "Young People's Magazine for Education and Recreation" announced a new novel by Jules Verne for the beginning of the year 1865 which had an amazing title *Journey to the Center of the Earth*.

The new novel was the only completely improbable fantasy of Jules Verne's entire output. It will never "come true" and will remain pure fantasy forever. Yet even this work of pure fiction exerted considerable influence on his contemporaries and opened up new fields of endeavor for many explorers, scientists, and authors.

Up to now Verne's heroes had been Englishmen, Americans, and Frenchmen. Now he chose a German minerologist named Professor Liedenbrock for his principal character. Liedenbrock discovered a sixteenth-century manuscript written by an alchemist who claimed that it was possible to reach the center of the earth through huge subterranean caves, provided one started the descent through the crater of a certain volcano in Iceland. Liedenbrock and his nephew, Axel, decide to follow the alchemist's plan. From the moment they find an Icelandic guide to lead them to the entrance of the cave, the fantastic adventures of the three men become progressively more breathtaking.

Again Jules Verne had hit on a new field of scientific investigation — the mysterious subterranean caves which were completely unknown to most of his readers. Together with Professor Liedenbrock we painfully descend through a narrow granite shaft which leads us further and further down, lose our way in the utter darkness, and finally reach a large, impassable subterranean lake. Huge ferns and mushrooms grow in the cold humidity.

Finally, by the light of their specially constructed lamps, the three find bones and skeletons

of prehistoric animals. A whole prehistoric landscape opens up before them. Since they cannot
continue their journey on foot, they build a barge
from the remains of ancient, almost petrified, logs.
They hope to travel over the subterranean seas
and streams in this bulky craft. Science had long
known about these subterranean oceans and
streams, but nobody had ever set eyes on them.
The first to see them, at least in their imaginations, would be Jules Verne's readers.

As the explorers go deeper, the temperature
gets warmer and warmer. Huge cavernous halls
and stalactite grottoes open up before them, bathed
in a seemingly magic twilight, the origin of which
remains a mystery even though it obviously
comes through cracks in the rock. Finally, far
below sea level, they reach an area of luxuriant
wild palms, cypresses, and creeping plants. The
professor realizes that the landscape here in the
lower strata of the earth had survived from prehistoric times.

In a clearing, the three men encounter a herd
of mastodons with huge tusks and snake-like
trunks — prehistoric monsters. At the last possible moment of safety, they escape unnoticed
to their barge and continue their journey — at
least for a while. Just when they start traveling at
a satisfactory rate of speed, huge masses of lava
stone block their way in all directions.

The three make ready to dynamite the blocks of
lava. But the explosion turns out to be a catas-
trophe. Suddenly an abyss opens up, the waters
gush into it and drag their barge along with the
speed of an express train. They race past walls of
rocks. This hellish journey lasts for hours, until
the barge suddenly and unexpectedly rises up.
The heat becomes unbearable and the water begins to boil. Even in this dangerous moment Professor Liedenbrock still keeps his presence of
mind. He attempts to explain the natural phe-
nomena by assuming that they must be right in
the midst of a volcanic eruption. And he is right.
All around them the sound of heavy explosions
repeats itself, then fades to a rumbling thunder.

The barge catapults upward with incredible
speed, through sulphurous flames and through a
rain of ashes, and then the three men are thrown
up into the air. At last they find themselves, half
unconscious, at the foot of a mountain.

Where are they? This cannot be Iceland. Above
them, the warm sun shines in a blue Mediterranean
sky. Finally they meet a tanned boy, and from
him they learn the name of the mountain. It is the
volcano "Stromboli" on an island off the southern
coast of Italy. They have traveled clear through
the center of the earth!

In the novel, Professor Liedenbrock is elected
an honorary member of many scientific societies,

but in the real world he was reviled by scientists who earnestly declared that the contents of this book was utter, untenable nonsense. The book drew worldwide attention to the existence of the huge caves. Soon the public began searching out the few existing articles on cave explorations, and in August 1922, a young Frenchman, Norbert Casteret, made a discovery of extraordinary significance.

He ventured through a dark passageway in a cave that he was exploring near the little village of Montespan in the Pyrenees. He came upon a huge hall. It was completely dark in this cavern, and from its ceiling moisture dripped to the rocky floor in a regular rhythm. By the light of his lantern, Casteret was able to discover that there was an upper story to his hall, and that a labyrinth of narrow corridors began at its far end.

Casteret could not advance very far because most of the corridors were flooded. But the next year Casteret returned with a friend during the dry season. They found the likenesses of tiny wild horses, mastodons, and bisons scratched into the walls of the hall. These animals had disappeared from Europe many, many centuries ago — no one but Stone Age men could have seen these creatures alive. Casteret and his friend had discovered one of the caves where prehistoric man had worshiped. For the first time the vivid, dra-

matic evidence of a culture many thousands of
years old could be seen by modern man. And
Casteret found even more. He discovered tools
used by men who had lived there 20,000 years
before, and a huge clay sculpture of a bear.

Once again Jules Verne had surmised the truth.
Prehistoric animals were indeed discovered in these
subterranean caves, although they were fortunately not alive as were those discovered by
Professor Liedenbrock! Cave exploration became
the rage after Casteret's first finds, and 115 hitherto
unknown caves with prehistoric paintings have
been discovered since then.

Casteret's daredevil expeditions gave new impetus to cave exploration in the south of France.
He discovered that subterranean caves ran the
entire width of the Pyrenees. Bags containing dyes
which had been thrown into waters running
through the caves on the French side would later
turn up in a mountain stream on the *other side* of
the Pyrenees — on Spanish soil.

With the aid of modern technology, it has been
possible to penetrate to a depth almost 1,000 feet
below the Pyrenees. The explorations in the caves
of Pierre San Martin are particularly well known,
and it was there that the French cave explorer
Marcel Loubens fell to his death in 1952. A
huge subterranean lake was discovered there, and
beyond it a subterranean waterfall. The accounts

given by the members of the expedition about their experiences beneath the surface of the earth correspond exactly to the grandiose and gloomy atmosphere described in Jules Verne's novel. The gifted writer had been able to describe, with incomparable vividness, a landscape that he himself had never set eyes upon.

Like a man in a dream, Jules Verne began to work with a unique creative fever, with the strong and boundless enthusiasm of an artist who has finally found his way, and he was overjoyed that he could use all the diversified knowledge he had acquired to such good advantage.

A brief four years ago he had been an utterly unknown, unhappy, and unsuccessful stockbroker. Now he had made the breakthrough. His success was assured, and his name was on everybody's lips. His books could be found wherever books were sold all over Europe, and they were also avidly read across the ocean, in America. The improbable had become a reality, and his success was beyond anything he had ever dared to hope for. Only now was he able to catch his breath and to enjoy, if only for a short time, the fruits of his success.

In accordance with the wishes of Madame Honorine, the Vernes left the apartment in the *Rue Montparnasse* and moved into a lovely small house in Auteuil, an elegant Paris suburb. It was at this luxuriously furnished house that Verne began giving his famous weekly parties, attended by both his bohemian friends and by other famous authors — among them Dumas and George Sand. Often famous pianists would play on the concert grand in his drawing room. At last, Jules Verne was living the life of a distinguished and affluent man of letters.

When he wanted to take Madame Honorine out, money was no longer a consideration. They attended the impudently witty operettas by Jacques Offenbach, and the brilliant opening nights of the Grand Opera, in their own box. Afterward they would enjoy a late supper at the *Café Anglais*, the most expensive and luxurious restaurant in Paris. Jules Verne had arrived!

And yet, after enjoying this high living for a few months, Verne found that it no longer meant very much to him. He had no intention of losing himself in this kind of living. He was soon at work in his new attic study, which he furnished like a ship's cabin. Marine maps hung on the walls and a large globe stood in a corner. At last he was able to buy all the scientific books he wanted instead of borrowing them from the libraries. In his attic "cabin" surrounded by this new wealth of material, he wrote a geography of France as a means of relaxing. Then he began to make notes on a new story for Hetzel's magazine.

It was at this time that Jules Verne made one of
his own childhood dreams come true. He bought
himself a boat, a little yacht, and he docked the
Saint Michel at Le Crotoy, a beautiful little fishing
town at the mouth of the Somme River. Now he
was captain on his own ship! This first *Saint
Michel* was quite a modest vessel and not to be
compared with the magnificent yacht in which he
would later cross the Mediterranean.

From then on Le Crotoy became the summer
paradise of the whole family. The children were
naturally delighted with the *Saint Michel*. But
Madame Honorine soon found out that her husband loved best to be alone on his ship, and since
she did not care much about sailing herself, she
was glad to let him have his pleasure. She was
happy that he found such a healthy counterbalance
to the many sedentary hours spent in his study.
She had as yet no inkling that the captain's cabin
on the *Saint Michel* had also become a workroom and that Captain Verne could be found
there much more frequently than on deck.

The second wish that came true in 1866 was a
long journey which Jules took with his brother
Paul. Since childhood, Paul and he had shared a
passionate interest in the ocean and foreign lands.
Now they set out for America on the *Great
Eastern,* the largest ship in the world. This was to
be her last transatlantic crossing before she was

finally converted into a cable-laying steamer, and
Jules had loved her ever since he had watched her
being built during his honeymoon.

The brothers Verne sailed in March, and before
the *Great Eastern* had left Liverpool, Jules began
exploring every inch of her. The great mirrored
ballroom and the staterooms, which were as beau-
tifully furnished as drawing rooms, were sights
to be seen. The *Great Eastern* carried 4,000 persons, and its powerful paddle wheels measured
more than fifty feet in diameter; they were almost
as high as a tenement building. After a stormy
crossing, during which they became acquainted
with the Atlantic at its wildest, the brothers
reached New York early in April. In those days
there were no skyscrapers in Manhattan, and the
city made less of an impression on Jules Verne
than Liverpool had. But the large scale of American living captured his imagination. The brothers
visited a few American cities, and then traveled
to the Canadian border in order to see Niagara
Falls. The tremendous roaring and hissing of the
water made a tremendous impression on Jules
Verne: he had found a landscape after his own
heart.

When they returned on the *Great Eastern* at the
end of the month, Jules Verne had jotted down a
wealth of ideas for future novels. During the return voyage Jules Verne once more experienced

the ocean, spending whole nights on deck in order
to observe the sea and the sky. On the other
hand, he enjoyed the luxury of the ship, the many
celebrations on board, and the social tempo of the
international set.

Upon his return he immediately set to work on
a new novel in the summer paradise of Le Crotoy.
This story begins with an ocean voyage, and it
was to appear in so many editions that royalties
from this book alone would have provided the
author with a comfortable living. *Captain Grant's
Children* was to become the most famous book
for young people he had yet written.

The adventures of these children take them
from England to South America and then to Aus-
tralia and New Zealand. One exciting episode fol-
lows another in swift succession, so that one can
hardly bear to put it down, but it is a first-rate
textbook of geography and history before the
mid-1800's to boot. It begins with a famous opening scene which would later on be imitated again
and again by countless authors: a letter is found in
a bottle. It contains a mysterious, mutilated text
in three languages.

When Jules Verne had completed *Captain
Grant's Children,* he was beset by a strange mood
of unrest. He talked to no one, not even to his
publisher, Hetzel, about his new plans. He envisioned a novel which would revolve around the

ocean, or rather which would be about *all* the oceans of the world. He had gathered thousands of notes on the subject. He wanted to tell about the secrets of the ocean, about its fishes and its treasures. He thought of stories about pearl fishers that he had tracked down in scientific journals, and then again of stories about sunken ships. His wealth of scientific material was tremendous, but he could not think of a plot that would enable him to use the thousands of interesting details that he wished to include.

Once again he could be found more often in the libraries than at home. One evening Madame Honorine waited for him in vain in her best ball gown. He had forgotten the festivities to which he had planned to take her, and sat instead at the Scientific Press Club, deeply involved in a technical discussion.

For a while, he planned a plot that would take place in the mysterious Sargasso Sea, with its floating isles of seaweed. Then he changed his mind and began to study all the technical innovations in shipbuilding, and also the story of all the inventors who had ever attempted to build submarines. He studied modern diving equipment, which was still so cumbersome and heavy that people laughed at it. In those days, divers did not dive very deep, and most of them worked in river harbors rather than in the ocean depths.

In the course of his research, Verne became more and more impatient. The ocean — such a gigantic subject! A story about the ocean would have to be a masterpiece. He had written his last novel quickly and easily, but now he had a deep urge to create on a large canvas — to create something extraordinary, no matter how long it took.

It was pure chance that brought about the happy instant in which he was suddenly able to envision the plot of his new novel, the account of still another extraordinary journey which had never before been described.

Early in December he gave a big party. The guests were mostly prominent people in the theatrical, operatic, and literary circles. Among them was the eccentric George Sand, infamous for her love affairs and even more so because she liked to appear in men's clothes, wearing a top hat on her long brown tresses. This time, however, she had not appeared in pants and a colorful vest, but was elegantly dressed in women's clothes. She was sipping a glass of champagne and conversing with her host when a random remark made by her in jest suddenly gave him the impetus for which he had been waiting so impatiently.

"You know, Verne," the lady novelist said laughingly when he told her about some of his new ideas, "in your books virtually anything can happen. I suppose one of these days you will succeed in making one of these ridiculous divers with their horrid diving costume a hero in a novel!"

"Divers," that was the key world for Verne — divers on the floor of the ocean, who could see what no man had ever yet set eyes on.

A few weeks later Verne decided to go to Le Crotoy, even though it was the middle of January. He wished to see absolutely nobody, and to spend his days on board his yacht. In the cold and stormy winter nights he gave birth to his great plan about which he continued to preserve a stubborn silence. This time it took him almost six months to rearrange and supplement his scientific material. Never before had he worked with such great care.

And then in the silent cabin on the *Saint Michel*, the lonely captain began to write. His "hero" was a misanthrope who had loosened all the ties that bound him to life on earth, and who roamed the fathomless depths of the oceans in a "submarine."

Jules Verne had started to write *Twenty Thousand Leagues Under the Sea* — his masterpiece, the greatest creation of his life.

5 THE MASTERPIECE

ONCE AGAIN, Jules Verne started a novel with the announcement of a fictitious event. He wrote of a mysterious monster that roams the oceans and that had already rammed several ships. Both seamen and scientists are exceedingly perplexed. Could this perhaps be a huge whale? Because the safety of all international shipping is endangered by the monster, a decision is made to hunt it down. A United States vessel is fitted out with harpooning equipment and sent off to bring this strange sea monster to bay.

Ned Land, the best harpooner to be found anywhere, is on board, and the United States government has invited a famous oceanographer and explorer, Professor Arronax from Paris, to join the expedition. Professor Arronax has just returned to New York from a scientific expedition to the Far West. He and his Flemish boy servant, Conseil, board the vessel just before its departure.

After many weeks of fruitless searching, they finally sight the sea monster somewhere in the Pacific. To their amazement, the curious, spindle-shaped monster travels much faster than the ships and emits an inexplicably strong ray of light as it plows through the waves. They shoot at it with a cannon, but the cannon ball hits the mysterious animal and rebounds. When the monster comes dangerously close to the ship, Ned Land hurls his harpoon, but it, too, strikes the creature without penetrating its hide.

At that moment there is a heavy collision, and the harpooner, the professor, and his servant are thrown into the sea. The vessel turns and flees, and it is doubtful whether anyone on board has noticed the disappearance of the three men in the general excitement.

The shipwrecked men are able to save their lives by hanging on to a small cliff. But the "cliff" turns out to be man-made steel plate, which is part of the mysterious monster. The monster is actually a huge submarine. No author had ever before conceived of such an idea, and it created even more of a sensation than Verne's moon rocket.

Suddenly the submarine begins to glide away, faster and faster. The three men on the slippery, narrow platform are surrounded by hissing and foaming waves and have to exert all their strength in order to hold on. Just as the waves threaten to carry them off, one of the plates is suddenly pushed back. Eight husky masked men appear and pull the harpooner and the two Frenchmen into the interior of the boat!

They are shut up in a small dark cell, which is suddenly flooded by blinding light, as the mysterious captain of the ship appears to question them. Captain Nemo decides to allow his uninvited guests to remain on board, but only under one condition: they will remain his prisoners as long as the *Nautilus* travels through the seas. Never again will they set foot on firm land, or return to the world of men.

After the first shock of this announcement has worn off a little, the three men are confronted with one surprise after another. They are taken on a tour of the submarine and find that it is furnished more comfortably than the most luxurious ocean liner. Its machinery is so modern that it surpasses every previous achievement of modern technology.

The captain shows the professor into a large library, thickly carpeted with bright, luxurious rugs, where 12,000 volumes are tightly crammed into the shelves. The drawing room beyond it is a veritable museum, with valuable paintings on the walls and genuine antique sculptures. An enormous concert grand stands in the background. In the center of the room, arranged around a brilliantly lit fountain, stand illuminated glass cases containing a fabulous collection of sea plants, sea animals, and other rarities. Professor Arronax is shown one scientific marvel after another — wonders that leave even today's readers dumbfounded.

Finally, Captain Nemo offers the Professor a cigar; it tastes like a fine Havana, but it is made from a certain type of seaweed! Products of the sea have been used in ways never thought of before: the rugs in the library had been dyed with colors produced by a sea snail, and all the ingredients of the excellent dinner are derived solely from the ocean. On the menu, which has been printed on board ship, Monsieur Arronax is amazed to find these dishes among many others:

Liver of dolphin
Turtle filet
A cream dessert made with whale milk
Compote of sea cucumber

The delicious fresh vegetables are all prepared from different kinds of seaweed. Readers in 1870 might well have been amazed and even revolted to read the *Nautilus'* menu. For who in those days knew that the Japanese had long since used seaweed as a vegetable — who, that is, except a few scientists and Jules Verne? Today we can learn from any encyclopedia that nutritional experts have long been working with seaweed, trying to convert it into a palatable dietary supplement. Seaweed flour has already been used as fodder for animals because of its high protein content. The important Vitamins C and K are also derived from seaweed, as well as a kind of sugar. Today we look toward marine plants and tiny marine animals as a means of providing additional food for our constantly increasing world population. In so doing, we are following in the footsteps of Captain Nemo.

Of all the scenic wonders aboard the *Nautilus*, Professor Arronax and his companions are most amazed by the constant and brilliant illumination. There is not even a dark corner anywhere aboard. Captain Nemo explains that the source of the submarine's light is electricity. The ship's engine is driven by electricity, and it is even possible to charge the entire hull of the boat with electricity. Electric wires heat the distilling apparatus that furnishes drinking water and also provides hot water for bathing. Electric pumps operate the diving chambers. The Captain derives his electricity directly from the ocean. He therefore does not need any conventional fuel and can remain under water for months at a time. Fresh air and a pleasant temperature are provided by the oxygen supply apparatus and by air conditioning.

And all this in the year 1870!

In those days, electrically heated water seemed an incomprehensible miracle, and air conditioning could not really be imagined by a generation familiar only with fireplaces and tile stoves. The fact that the *Nautilus* could travel under water for months — even 20,000 miles if necessary — without surfacing for fuel, was simply accepted as the wildest fantasy! It would take ninety years to make this fantasy come true!

What contemporary readers found most exciting was the magic word "electricity." This really set their imaginations going. Little was known, then, about this new force, but the word alone had an effect like magic, for it sounded so incredibly modern. Electric motors, electric clocks, electric light that could shine even more brightly than the new gas lamps — impossible! Eleven years later, at the Paris World's Fair in 1881, Thomas Edison's incandescent bulb was first demonstrated, and another of Jules Verne's "inventions" had become a reality.

The great success of the amazing opening chapters of *Twenty Thousand Leagues Under the Sea* was due to the fact that all of the fabulous inventions Verne pictured were believable because of the giant technological strides being made each day by scientists. The fresh air pumps, the diving suits, and the submarine harpoons — all these things could be visualized so accurately by Verne's readers that they could not help asking: Why aren't these inventions on the market? Engineers and scientists soon asked themselves the same question. Tempted by the fascinating inventions of Verne's novel, they began to calculate and to experiment. But Verne was a step ahead of the scientists again. Having dazzled his readers with marvelous new technological advances, he now turned to the sea itself for new wonders.

Professor Arronax is relaxing in the elongated drawing room of the *Nautilus*, which is swiftly gliding along beneath the surface of the sea, when all the lamps suddenly go out. Gradually, however, light seems to filter in from the outside. The steel plates that form the room's two long walls glide noiselessly back, and now on either side only two huge, thick crystal windows separate the interior of the drawing room from the electrically illuminated ocean depths.

Professor Arronax and his companions see the teeming life of the ocean in the clear water surrounding them. Swarms of rare, exotic fish travel slowly past the windows. Sharks, rays, and barbels stare into the vessel; mackerel, carps, and eels pass in ever-changing shapes and colors.

This is indeed the fulfillment of an oceanographer's dream: to glide all in comfort through the most tremendous aquarium imaginable — the depths of the Pacific Ocean!

And yet, improbable as it sounds, Professor Arronax would be able to observe the inhabitants of the ocean and even the ocean floor from still greater proximity. The sixteenth chapter bears the exciting, amusing title: "A Walk on the Bottom of the Sea."

Certainly the imagination of this Monsieur Verne was boundless! For their excursion, Captain Nemo and Professor Arronax don a completely new kind of diving equipment. Through an ingenious system of sluices, the two gentlemen can travel from the interior of the ship directly to the ocean floor.

They are able to move — and this is indeed amazing — with complete freedom and without cumbersome air hoses; all they have to do is turn on their breathing apparatus. They carry this breathing apparatus on their backs, just as divers wear aqualungs today. The men have strong electric lamps attached to their belts, and each of them carries a "submarine rifle," an air gun that shoots small glass pellets charged with a fatal electric current. (This was an Austrian invention that

Jules Verne had picked up in the course of his reading and had utilized here.)

The submarine walk on the fine sand of the ocean's floor now begins. The gentlemen move at exactly the depth that is now known to be the ideal hunting grounds for submarine sportsmen: thirty feet below the surface. Here the sunlight still shines brightly. The plants, shells, and polyps in these submarine rock gardens glow in a magnificent medley of greens, yellows, and purples. Schools of fish and squid glide through the water above the walking men. Soon they are walking through a meadow of seaweed and reach a forest of huge coral. By the light of their lamps they observe a domain "in which the animal kingdom blossoms and the flora resembles the fauna." Tiny fish dart about like birds flying from shrub to shrub in a forest. But dangers also lurk here; a huge sea spider approaches them and has to be killed with a blow from the butt end of a gun. Now they descend a steep incline and the darkness deepens. At the depth of 450 feet their excursion is halted by a huge, steep rock.

During the return trip, Captain Nemo shoots a large sea otter with his air gun—a hunting venture on the bottom of the ocean! But soon afterward, the captain pushes the professor down to the ground and signals to him that he is to remain motionless. Hidden in the shade of a seaweed bush, Professor Arronax stares at the two tremendous sharks that pass over them, so close that they brush against them with their brownish fins. Fortunately, this incident ends without mishap.

Among all the sciences in the book, however, there was one in particular that captured the imagination of readers everywhere. It became the subject of countless discussions in the clubs. Many took every word very seriously, as though it were gospel truth. And we shall see that they were not so very much mistaken at that!

The chapter in question is the one which describes the treasures to be found on the ocean floor. The readers were fascinated by the ghostly fleet of treasure ships that had been sunk in the course of centuries, containing jewels and bars of gold and silver worth millions of dollars, and about which Captain Nemo was so very well informed.

In the second volume of *Twenty Thousand Leagues Under the Sea*, the *Nautilus* stops at Vigo Bay off the Spanish Coast. In accordance with historical fact, twenty-three Spanish galleons, sunk on October 22, 1702, were lying there filled with treasure.

"The saloon was dark," Professor Arronax explains in the novel, "but through the crystal plates the waves sparkled. For a half mile around the *Nautilus* the water was brightly illuminated.

On the sandy bottom stood some of the ship's crew in their diving suits, engaged in emptying half-rotten barrels and battered cases; ingots of gold and silver, piastres (coins) and jewels cascaded through their hands and found their way into the *Nautilus*. So it was here that Captain Nemo stocked up the millions with which he burdened the *Nautilus*."

In the course of his solitary journeys beneath the surface of the sea, Captain Nemo had discovered most of the sunken vessels containing treasure, and had made an accurate chart of all these wrecks. Among them are the wrecks of ancient Roman galleys in the Mediterranean, from which he had acquired his precious antique statues.

Captain Nemo's imaginary map, charting the positions of wrecks lying on the bottom of the sea, has now actually been drawn up. Explorers and scientists have compiled it after long cooperative efforts, and new information is still being added as it is obtained.

We shall only mention one of the modern treasure seekers: Lieutenant Harry Rieseberg. This American has compiled a list of almost five hundred treasure ships that have been sunk, and he has visited most of them. In the course of seven years he has salvaged old coins and gold ingots valued at $135,000.

Above all, the exploration of the world below

the surface of the sea, from the coral forests down to the greatest ocean depths, was fully realized only after long and arduous preliminary efforts. The things Jules Verne had described so vividly in his book had inspired the imagination of a few individuals. Just as one day it would be possible to build a perfect *Nautilus*, so would it be possible to observe life below sea level through thick crystal windows, though perhaps in somewhat less comfortable surroundings than those of Professor Arronax in Verne's novel.

The first modern submarine was built only twenty-eight years after the publication of Verne's novel. It was built by Simon Lake, an American, who himself said that he had constructed a vessel "every bit the *Nautilus*." But the purpose of this realization of the *Nautilus* was not the observation of the submarine world; from the very beginning it was destined for war and destruction. The exploration of the depths of the sea would in reality be achieved in a very different way than the one conceived and so marvelously described by Jules Verne.

In the beginning of June 1930, an American exploratory vessel stopped in the tropical waters near the Bermudas. On deck rested a peculiar apparatus — a huge steel sphere weighing 5,000 pounds, with three thick quartz windows.

William Beebe, the great American explorer and

an avid Jules Verne fan, had ordered this sphere
to be built after countless experiments. He and
its builder, Otis Barton, squeezed into the sphere
and once more tested the equipment, the search-
lights, and the camera. Then the steel door, weighing 360 pounds, was put in place and tightly
sealed. Attached to a thick steel cable 3,500 feet
long, the deep-sea sphere was hauled overboard.
What had once fascinated William Beebe as a
twelve-year-old boy reading Jules Verne's novel,
he would now be able to see with his own eyes.

It was also William Beebe who, long before this
diving experiment, was the first to walk below
the surface of the ocean on an underwater reef.
For this he did not use any cumbersome diving
equipment, and ventured down wearing only
swimming trunks, a pair of play shoes with rubber
soles, and a copper helmet with a glass insert. He
obtained the air for breathing by means of an
ordinary rubber hose and a small manual pump.
At a depth of about thirty-six feet he wandered
through coral gardens with sea anemones, sea stars,
large shrimps, huge snails, and pipefish. Beebe
even took notes under water on tin sheets, and
made drawings standing on the ocean floor at an
easel weighted with lead. Verne would have re-
joiced at this.

The example of Dr. Beebe incited others to
further exploration, and thus underwater observa-

tion was followed by submarine hunting and finally by underwater photography. A fellow countryman of Jules Verne, Captain Jacques-Yves Cousteau, was to go further down into the depths of the ocean than any other manfish. Equipped only with a mask, an aqualung on his back, and rubber fins on his feet, he was able to go down 270 feet below the surface.

Swimming among schools of fish, he could observe how they communicated with one another, penetrate underwater caves, and feel his way around wrecks covered with algae and barnacles. Just like Captain Nemo he carried an "underwater rifle" for protection—a special kind of harpoon about two yards long with an explosive point.

But in one thing he went beyond Captain Nemo and Professor Arronax. He captured the secrets of the submarine world with a camera. He was the first person to take flash-bulb photographs in the eternal colorless dusk 150 feet below the surface. These belong to the most sensational pictorial documents ever made. The glare of the reflector suddenly reveals in the darkness as he described them, "a carnival of colors, in which exuberant tones of red and orange predominate as in a painting by Matisse!"

It is not possible to enumerate here all the amazing scenes and adventures to be found in *Twenty Thousand Leagues Under the Sea*. They finally culminate in the discovery of the South Pole by Captain Nemo. The *Nautilus* traveled underneath the ice pack to reach the Pole, a marvelous scene envisioned by Jules Verne's vivid imagination, which would later on become reality.

Jules Verne celebrated New Years Eve 1868 with his publisher, Hetzel, at the *Rue Jacob*. On that occasion he handed over about 150 pages of his submarine novel.

It is easy to imagine Hetzel's enthusiasm once he had read those pages! When he learned that the *Nautilus* would continue to roam through the seven seas, circle around Asia, cross beneath the Isthmus of Suez, and navigate through the Gulf Stream, encountering countless adventures en route, the publisher realized that this book would probably be the most successful of all. Soon everybody would be talking about the *Nautilus* and Captain Nemo, as though they were discussing well-known facts.

Thus Hetzel decided that the book edition of this new novel would be illustrated with very special care. He suggested that Jules Verne furnish the sketches, which he did with great enthusiasm, and that he also approve each wood engraving upon its completion. The work on the illustrations alone took a whole year.

6 HIS GREATEST SUCCESS

THE PREVIOUS YEAR, 1869, had marked the completion of two tremendous technological undertakings which many had believed impossible to achieve. On May 10, the construction of the Union-Pacific Railway had been completed. The United States had commissioned two different companies to build this gigantic new railway, which was to cross the entire North American continent and extend about 3,300 miles through the prairies and the Rocky Mountains. In a competitive fever, two forces of engineers and laborers worked toward each other from East and West, from the Atlantic to the Pacific, across the entire width of the continent. When the rails were joined in Fort Laramie, the work had been completed

almost five years sooner than estimated. In spite
of tornadoes and terrible prairie fires, in spite of
the hostile Indians and the difficulties posed by
the Rocky Mountains, the connection between
East and West had been achieved. Now people
could travel from the Atlantic to the Pacific Ocean
by railroad.

November of the same year marked the opening
of the Suez Canal. It had taken ten long years of
dredging and building to create this new navigation route, which would shorten the distance from
Europe to India by about 4,400 miles — twenty-
four days of travel. In order to dig and fortify this
steamship route, millions of cubic feet of sand
and stone had to be dislodged under the most
adverse conditions and in a murderously hot cli-
mate. That the work on this gigantic project
could be completed at all was due to the unprece-
dented and tireless energy of its builder, Ferdinand
de Lesseps. And when the Suez Canal was finally
opened on November 17, 1869, by the French
Empress Eugénie, the newspapers celebrated this
moment as the most consequential event since the
discovery of America, and de Lesseps was hailed
as the greatest Frenchman of his time.

Early in January 1870, Jules Verne's *Twenty
Thousand Leagues Under the Sea* appeared. The
excellent artistic quality of the illustrations alone
caused a minor sensation. One of the first readers

of the book was de Lesseps, and in February this
great engineer proposed Jules Verne for the
Legion of Honor, France's highest tribute to her
most distinguished citizens. This was indeed fabulous recognition for an author. But it soon became
evident that the whole world agreed with de
Lesseps.

The publication of his books had made Jules
Verne famous as the author of the new era and,
even more than that, had gained him recognition
as the prophet of the age of technology. The
avalanche of success which came from his
Twenty Thousand Leagues Under the Sea circled
the entire globe and reached readers of every sort.
But while Jules Verne was being celebrated abroad
as the foremost author of science fiction, the author shared in the distressing events that were
taking place in his fatherland—the fall of the
Empire, the siege of Paris by German armies,
and the riots of the Commune in the French
capitol—for July 1870 marked the beginning of
the disastrous Franco-Prussian War.

The outbreak of the war surprised Jules Verne
on his yacht *Saint Michel*. He and his family were
spending the summer at Le Crotoy. Up there, at
the mouth of the Somme, there was no danger of
any Prussian attack, nor was the forty-two-year-
old Jules Verne subject to military draft.

But the unrest of the times reached even to the

most remote corners of the country. The military
commander of the coastal area wished to make
his contribution to the glory and security of
France. He sent twelve veterans to the *Saint Michel*
and incorporated Captain Jules Verne and
his yacht into the "coast guard," presumably in
the expectation that the vicious Prussians had secretly acquired a fleet of warships and would
launch their attack on France at Le Crotoy. It
took several weeks before this extremely cautious
measure was abandoned.

While the French capital suffered the terrible
winter's siege of 1870-71, Jules Verne remained
on his yacht. His family went to Madame Honorine's hometown, Amiens. Verne threw himself
into his work with such intensity that by spring
he had completed four new manuscripts. He was
shocked and disgusted by the war, and distressed
at France's capitulation. The only good thing he
could see in it was that the Republic would now
prevail after the questionable sovereignty of the
Empire.

As soon as the armistice was signed, in May of
the next year, Jules Verne immediately set out for
Paris. The streets were still unsafe. Some districts
were ruled by the rabble. Many of those who
had fled Paris during the war had not yet returned,
and Verne was unable to find Hetzel, who had
fled the intrigues and accusations of the Commune

and gone to the Riviera—address unknown. In the *Rue Jacob*, Verne found all the blinds drawn. Hetzel's printers and other employees were still in the army.

Verne had not counted on Hetzel's absence, and he urgently needed cash. Only now did he realize how carefree he had been in the management of his affairs. There hardly remained anything of the large sums he had received.

What could he do, beyond selling some jewelry and furniture, in order to be able to send his family money? In his suitcase he had four completed manuscripts; their titles were already known to Hetzel. To offer them to another publisher meant endangering his contract with Hetzel. There was only one way out: to write a new novel as fast as possible, and to get one of the large Paris dailies to print it in installments before the appearance of the regular book edition. But where could he quickly find an exciting subject, which would interest everyone even in these difficult days?

It was a peculiar situation for the famous author, a predicament reminiscent of his youth. As in his student days, he once more roamed alone through the streets of Paris and sat around in cafés in search of an idea!

One late spring day, when Jules Verne passed through the *Boulevard des Italiens* not far from the opera house, he chanced to stop in front of the display window of Thomas Cook and Son, the travel agency. Even in those days Cook's was the largest travel agency in the world, and it had just published a new prospectus. After his long, involuntary confinement on the *Saint Michel*, Jules was more in the mood for travel than ever before. He asked for a copy of the prospectus and took it along to the *Café Tortoni*.

Cook was the originator of the convenient "group tour." Since 1841, his travel agencies had organized "trips" for their customers. No matter where one might wish to go — to Greece, Norway, India, or Mexico — one only had to pay for a book of Cook coupons, and all the problems of the journey were solved in advance. The little book of Cook coupons contained all the needed tickets, hotel reservations, and vouchers that entitled the holder to the services of guides and interpreters.

Cook's new prospectus pointed out the convenience of the newly completed railroad line, the Union-Pacific, which provided the fastest connection between San Francisco and New York. It also mentioned the new steamship route through the Suez Canal to India. Tickets for all these new connections could be purchased at Cook's; and if one were inclined to make a trip all around the world, it would now be possible to do it in only three months!

A trip around the world in ninety days. This extravagant claim by Thomas Cook and Son gave wings to Jules Verne's imagination.

Surely the claim was not just idly made. But was it really possible to make all those connections on time? And what would be the result of any delay that might occur? Was it even remotely possible to go around the world in even less time than stipulated by Cook?

To make such a trip — stopwatch in hand — that would really be something! Jules Verne was reminded of his strict and punctilious father, who had calculated the distance to his office or to the docks not merely by the clock, but even by counting the number of his strides.

At one o'clock that night, when the waiters of the *Café Tortoni* began to put the chairs up on the tables and to extinguish the elegant gas lamps, they found the slender gentleman with the brown beard, who looked like a captain in civilian clothes, still sitting at a little marble table in the corner, scribbling line after line in a small notebook.

That night, in a café on one of the Parisian boulevards, the idea was born for the most successful novel of the nineteenth century, *Around the World in Eighty Days*, and with it was born a new kind of contemporary hero — Phileas Fogg!

The book had appeared in innumerable editions, was at one time acted on the stage all over Europe, and has recently been revived in a movie. The novel is a classical document of the infancy of the age of technology. It is not out of date even today, when we can circle the globe in much less time by airplane.

In less than two weeks, Jules Verne had outlined the story and offered it to the Paris newspaper *Temps* for serial publication. Even in these turbulent times the editors welcomed the now famous author. As soon as the gentlemen of the *Temps* heard the title, they grabbed at the chance to serialize the book and gave Verne a fabulous sum to assure their paper's priority.

They would have no cause for complaint. Never before had such a fireworks of exciting adventures appeared on their fiction page. Episodes followed one another without any let-up in pace; nothing could be guessed in advance, and everything turned out quite differently from what the reader expected. *Around the World in Eighty Days* became the most successful serial novel ever to be published.

The opening episode of the book — the wager made at the Reform Club in London — caused such a sensation among its readers that they, too, began to bet on the odds that Fogg would, or would not, make the journey in eighty days. Phileas Fogg's perpetual composure delighted the public, as did his companion, the always cheerful Passepartout.

The ingenious inventions of the detective, Mr. Fix, ever in pursuit of Fogg, kept everyone in an ecstasy of suspense.

As soon as the first installments began to appear they were such a success that the *Temps* now gained subscribers even in the most distant provinces of France, and in England. But the Americans also wanted to read this serial novel. Finally, the Paris correspondents of the foreign dailies were obliged to cable the contents of the latest installment to their respective papers every day. Short summaries of the action appeared daily in the New York and San Francisco papers. Readers in England and in America read the summary of an installment and then hurried to a booking agent to place their bets either for or against Fogg's making the trip in eighty days. Perhaps these "pools" spurred Jules Verne on to invent even more suspenseful episodes. The *Temps* had not given him time to finish his manuscript before publication, and installments were already appearing while he was still writing the book.

The author kept his readers in an almost painful suspense. In San Francisco, exactly halfway through their journey around the world, Fogg and Passepartout had made up for all time losses. But this was only the beginning of a whirlwind trip across the North American continent, made, of course, on the new Union-Pacific Railroad.

Every installment brought another sensation, from a brawl in a wild-West bar to an Indian attack and Passepartout's capture. But, happen what might, Fogg had to be in New York by December 11 in order to make connections with the steamer to Europe, for otherwise he would not be able to appear at the Reform Club in time to collect his wager.

Never before had so many persons studied time-tables or deluged the branches of Cook's Travel Bureau with so many questions as during the days when Jules Verne's novel appeared serially in the *Temps*. While the whole world waited with bated breath to see whether Fogg would reach the steamer on time, the amount of the bets kept increasing. As Fogg approached New York, summaries of the current installment appeared on the front page of the evening papers. And then came the climax — Fogg had missed the steamer to Liverpool by forty-five minutes.

The editors of the *Temps* were deluged with a veritable flood of indignant letters. Four New York shipping firms, however (among them the White Star and the Cunard Lines), immediately perceived a marvelous opportunity for publicity. Independent of one another, they cabled Jules Verne in Paris, offering him a large sum of money if he would let Fogg return on one of their ships.

Jules Verne laughingly declined. Now Jules

Verne played on the nerves of his readers to the utmost. Readers who had placed high bets in favor of Fogg were in despair when Mr. Fix, the detective, managed at the last minute to arrest the great traveler and have him thrown into prison.

Now Fogg could not possibly win the wager. Indeed, he arrived in London five minutes late. But the novel was not yet at an end, and Jules Verne had a last trick up his sleeve.

Fogg had not taken into consideration that, since his trip around the world was made from West to the East, he had gained a full twenty-four hours. He arrived home ahead of London time by an entire day.

Just before the expiration of this twenty-four hours' grace, Fogg learns this fact from his devoted servant, Passepartout. He leaps into a carriage and enters the smoking room of the Reform Club at the stroke of seven o'clock, exactly eighty days after he had left it!

Two years later, when the book had been dramatized and had appeared as a very successful stage play in all the main European cities, it was this final scene that always called forth the greatest applause and stole the show. Phileas Fogg would appear in the Reform Club, resplendent in full evening clothes. He would nonchalantly remove his hat and remark offhandedly to his dumbfounded companions: "Well, gentlemen, here I am!"

In Paris, the stage adaptation of *Around the World in Eighty Days* ran for over a year. In France alone the play brought in more than three million gold francs. In a completely different way than he had once envisioned, Jules Verne now achieved his early dream: He had become a successful playwright.

Like Jules Verne's earlier books, *Around the World in Eighty Days* fired people's imaginations and spurred them on to imitation. Only a few years later, an ambitious American lady-reporter was able to better Fogg's record by eight days. This in turn spurred on an English colonel to make the trip around the world — in four days less than his predecessor. Finally a French journalist set a record by journeying around the world in forty-three days.

Even during the twentieth century the imitation of the hero of *Around the World in Eighty Days* has not lost its allure. When, in 1929, the whole world celebrated the hundredth anniversary of Jules Verne's birth, a Danish newspaper announced a youth contest for a trip around the world in eighty days. A fifteen-year-old boy scout won the prize.

And sixty-three years after the appearance of the novel, in 1936, a well-known French author,

Jean Cocteau, fulfilled a dream of his boyhood and followed in the footsteps of his favorite hero. He was not out to set another record for speed because he wanted to enjoy the experience to the hilt. Therefore, even though he used much more modern means of transportation than Phileas Fogg had had at his disposal, he nevertheless took fifty-seven days to complete his journey.

When today we once again read this still-popular novel, it drives home a new and unexpected point. For in one particular factor we lag shamefully behind Phileas Fogg. It does not take him more than an hour to be ready for a trip all around the world. He puts his passport in his pocket, throws 20,000 English pounds into his traveling bag, packs the necessary linen, and he's off!

And today? How many weeks would it take for Phileas Fogg just to obtain the necessary visas for the different countries of the Near and Far East? In addition, he would have to make various applications for foreign exchange permits, filling out all the needed questionnaires. Furthermore, he could not have left without being vaccinated against smallpox, typhoid, and malaria, and surely he would have missed many of his carefully calculated connections waiting to have his baggage inspected by the customs officers of each county.

Jules Verne now counted his readers in the

millions; his works, which had long since been
translated into the chief languages of the world,
now appeared even in Persian and Chinese. His
daily mail brought fan letters and inquiries from
all over the world. He was the favorite author of
simple people and of many artists and scientists.
The Czar of Russia and Emperor William II were
among his admirers. Jules Verne, the unknown
romantic poet, who had at one time been obliged
to take a meager job at the *Théâtre Lyrique* in
order to drive away the pangs of hunger, had now
become the most famous French author of his
time.

During this second period of prolific creativity,
Jules Verne regaled his readers with a wealth of
"extraordinary travels," in which they could experience the greatness and the beauty of the wide
world, a world that was swiftly becoming mech-
anized. Jules Verne led his readers through the
jungle of the Amazon and up to the icy deserts of
Alaska, from the Ural Mountains to Hawaii and
Patagonia, and each of his books was an extraordinary tale of adventure, peopled with interesting
heroes.

In addition, his novels served as fascinating geographical textbooks and first-rate travel guides. No
matter whether he was writing about the phos-
phorescence of the ocean or flying fish, about the
South African lantern fly or a Canadian dog-sled

race, Jules Verne always gave all the details of geographical, anthropological, and scientific interest. His contribution to the "scientific novel" has never been equalled by any other writer.

One of these novels of travel and adventure is of very special significance, and in a selection of Jules Verne's writing it ought to be placed side by side with his masterpieces. This novel is entitled *The Mysterious Island*. The problem it treats of has as great an interest for today's readers as it had for the readers of 1880. This is the problem of a modern Robinson Crusoe. How would Crusoe act now, in the era of technology, if he were shipwrecked? What new aids to survival would he have at his disposal?

This novel begins when a balloon is caught in a hurricane of four days' duration, and is finally sucked into a water spout. Its five passengers appear to be doomed. The balloon sinks rapidly toward the hissing waves. Only at the last desperate moment are the travelers able to save themselves and land on the beach of a small island.

They find themselves on an uninhabited volcanic island. Five people, with an engineer, Cyrus Smith, at their helm, have been torn from modern civilization and, in their lonely and helpless condition, must contend with nature. For the moment, they have no technological aids at their disposal. But after calm and careful deliberation, the five begin to work; they take advantage of all favorable conditions afforded by nature, and they are able to surmount, one after another, the tremendous difficulties confronting them.

Never to lose one's head, never to give up, but to think calmly and attempt to make the best of even the most catastrophic predicament — this was the motto by which they survived. But the main reason for their success — and this is brought out here for the first time in a modern adventure story — is the fact that they work together deliberately as a team under the leadership of Cyrus Smith. Each man is utilized in accordance with his skills and physical strength. By pooling their resources they are able to survive and to create all the necessities of life on the island.

This concept of the "team" plays a decisive role in modern exploratory expeditions. The fact that Jules Verne's heroes were often exceptionally well informed, familiar with the most complicated chemical formulas and immediately able to identify all kinds of plants and rocks, was frequently made fun of. And yet it was because of his heroes' exceptional skills that Jules Verne's readers found them so interesting. And this is exactly how modern scientific teams are set up today. They consist of specialists, the knowledge of each member complimenting that of the others. Perhaps the most famous team of this sort is the English group that was able, by using each member's special skills, to first conquer Mount Everest.

There was still another, very immediate way in which *The Mysterious Island* affected our times. It established a precedent for the founding of training courses for modern "Crusoes," and in this age of constantly increasing air transportation, the problem of the modern Crusoe has become a very important one. Again and again, planes have been forced to make emergency landings in the jungles of the Amazon, in the lonely forests of Canada, and in great deserts and savannahs. Often their passengers have not survived. In these huge areas of difficult terrain, such downed planes have been as hard to spot as the proverbial needle in a haystack. Occasionally, it has happened — purely by chance — that the utterly exhausted passengers, on the verge of death and starvation, have been saved.

After Crusoe cases began to mount, one American had a marvelous idea. (In his library, incidentally, were all of Jules Verne's books, and he had studied *The Mysterious Island* with great care.) He suggested that air and naval crews be trained in advance for these Crusoe situations. At first he was laughed at. But since 1947 carefully planned training courses in survival have been held.

In one of the theoretical sessions a pilot was asked: "What would you do if you had to make an emergency landing in completely uninhabited terrain without any paths or roads?" He answered: "I would shoot a bullet through my head!" To combat this sort of attitude, groups of five young men — exactly the number of persons in Jules Verne's novel — were sent to uninhabited South Sea islands without any equipment. However, each group, in addition, included one native. This was a hard school, which lasted for fourteen long days. Later on the groups were enlarged to include ten men. Again they were provided with one trapper (or hunter, fisher, or mountaineer, depending on the type of terrain in which the group was left to fend for itself). After fourteen days, a helicopter or airplane would reappear to pick the men up.

These groups developed remarkable powers of invention in order to survive. They learned how to catch fish like the Indians, by anesthetizing them with vegetable poisons; on barren cliffs, they learned to live on birds and their eggs, and it was discovered that grasshoppers, larvae of beetles, mussels, seaweed, snakes, and burrowing animals were quite edible. The hides of animals could be pulled off and used for improvised sleds, in which the meat could be dragged to shelter. Drinking water could be obtained from lianas (rain-forest plants) in the jungle.

Furthermore, the trainees learned that even salt water is potable and that salt-water fish may be eaten raw without any ill effects. For cooking and baking, no pots and pans were necessary, for raw meat could be grilled on hot stones in a covering of mud. The adventures of these groups are vividly reminiscent of the happenings in Jules Verne's *Mysterious Island*.

A great traveler — that is how his readers imagine their favorite author. Once a group of London students presented him with an expensive bamboo cane, which, it was presumed, he would take on his world-wide excursions. On another occasion a footman brought Verne a comfortable chair as he waited in the antechamber of a Paris ministry. The footman explained his action by saying: "Surely you must be exhausted after your last journey, Monsieur Verne." From the newspapers, everyone learned that Verne had ordered the most modern French steam yacht — once again it was christened *Saint Michel* — and they imagined that he was constantly on the go in his new boat. It seemed unimaginable to his readers that Verne had never seen the places and things he described so vividly and accurately.

In the spring of 1884, Jules Verne really did embark on a long journey aboard the *Saint*

Michel. He was accompanied by his wife, his son, his brother, Paul, and one of his young nephews. He headed for the Mediterranean, and his trip was to become a triumphal cruise for the famous author. It seemed like something out of a fairy tale to Verne that he could now enter the harbor of Nantes at the helm of his own ship and berth at the very dock from which he had once, as a twelve-year-old boy, gazed so longingly at the sea and dreamed of far-off lands.

On his arrival in Tunis he received the first of many great honors. The bey (or governor) of Tunis was an enthusiastic reader of Jules Verne's books. He not only entertained Verne at his court but also arranged for a visit to Carthage, and placed his own luxurious private train at the disposal of his favorite author.

At Oran, the Geographical Society prepared a welcoming celebration for Jules Verne. On the island of Malta, the officers of the English fleet stationed in the harbor of Lavaletta hailed him by firing a salute in his honor. Soon afterward, the city of Rome gave a gala performance at the *Teatro Umberto,* followed by a grand dinner at the Farnese Palace. In Venice, he was welcomed with a magnificent display of fireworks, and the throng gave him such an accolade that he appeared on the balcony of his hotel to thank them.

But the greatest honor of all was an audience

with the Pope in the Vatican. All the newspapers gave it headlines. Pope Leo XIII spent more than an hour with the author, who in one of his books had conquered the heavens with a retro-rocket! He told Jules Verne that he had read almost all his works. "For me, the scientific aspect of your work is not the most important. I admire above all the moral and spiritual values expressed in your books." These values, which earned the praise of the head of the Catholic church, are the values of a man who wanted to employ technology and the conquest of natural forces to serve all of humanity, and to bring civilization to the furthest corners of the earth.

FOREBODINGS

THE CELEBRATED AUTHOR, whose technological imagination had invented miracles such as the moon rocket and the *Nautilus*, came to realize shortly after 1884 that the advances of technology could actually threaten humanity with great danger if they came into the hands of men without conscience.

After his Mediterranean journey Jules Verne shut himself up in his workroom in the tower at Amiens. He worked longer hours than usual and did not even come down for meals. He brought the completed manuscript to Paris and showed it to his publisher, Hetzel, who, for the first time, was doubtful.

But Verne had once again foreseen what was to

become a piece of reality later on. *The Begum's Fortune* was the title of his novel. In it he envisioned a prototype of Adolf Hitler. The book begins innocently enough when the gigantic treasure of a dead Indian princess comes into the possession of her two nephews, a German and a Frenchman. Herr Schulze, the German, has hatched a plan whereby the Germanic race is to become master of the universe at any cost. With his billions, he builds "Steel City," where he produces powerful new explosive missiles that have a hitherto unimaginable destructive force.

The Frenchman has in the meantime used his money to build France-Ville, a city of beauty and order, planned in accordance with the best findings of science. Large apartment houses rise on spacious green lawns, reminding us of the airy garden cities planned by our modern architects.

Long-range cannons of a new kind are set up in Steel City. They can propel missiles hundreds of miles, and the barrels are trained on France-Ville. Only at the last moment does the German plan fail.

In one of his next novels, Jules Verne envisions a world in which the different continents wage war against each other. A small group of civilized human beings attempts to save itself from destruction. Its engineers build a floating island for this purpose. This "Propeller Island" with its capital,

"Milliard-City," is a miracle of technology. Driven by huge motors, it travels through the oceans. But even here strife and fighting break out. The survivors finally take over a part of the city and head for New Zealand, where they hope to live in peace and tranquility.

A gruesome future is envisioned by Jules Verne in another of his books, *The Incredible Adventure of Barsack*. Its chief protagonist is a half-witted scientist named Camaret. He misuses science in order to persecute people. He found Blackland, a city in Africa that has a remarkable resemblance to Buchenwald, used as a German concentration camp in World War II. There are three classes in Blackland: the directors, the underlings, and the slaves. Science here is misused for the purpose of torturing people and for carrying out criminal experiments on human beings.

As an aging and increasingly lonely man, Jules Verne foresaw all the dangers inherent in a technology that is unleashed and used inhumanely. As a final monstrosity that can be produced by a technology no longer held in check by either culture or reason, his imagination created the *Fulgurator Roch*. This is a heavy, shapeless cannon, capable of hurling off an explosive bomb made "out of completely new substances." This bomb destroys all life within a radius of six miles. The atom bomb immediately comes to mind! And we find it "invented" by Jules Verne in a novel which first appeared in 1896!

Where is Verne's abounding optimism now? What has happened to the happy inventiveness that caused him to invent one technological wonder after another? It seems that Verne was able to foresee the future in every aspect — good and bad. The words of Captain Nemo, the great misanthrope, seem to echo Jules Verne's presentiments: "The world needs no new continents, it needs new men!"

More and more, the elderly Jules Verne preferred to remain in his small tower workroom at Amiens. During the last decade of the century, he hardly ever traveled to Paris except to visit the libraries and to confer with scientists and other experts. Wherever he did appear, the world-famous author became the center of attention. In the year 1886, his name was even suggested for the presidency of the Republic.

Public opinion has long since considered him the prophet of the age of technology. His books were given a place in the library of Oxford University. Only one great ambition remained unfulfilled: He was never elected a member of the Academy of Science. The young writers read his books and admired his imagination and creative powers, but the white-haired scholars and professors in the hallowed halls of the Academy in

Paris thought that they could smile condescend-
ingly at this "author of utopian sensationalism,"
and pass judgment on him.

Today most of these learned scholars are
known only to a small circle, while Jules Verne is
honored all over the world. The books by these
academicians have, for the greater part, passed
into utter oblivion, but the chief novels of Jules
Verne are still appearing in one edition after another.

If Jules Verne did not appeal to the theoreti-
cians, he was and is fully appreciated by men of
practical knowledge and men of action, who read
his works over and over again. Louis H. Lyautey,
who later became marshal of France, wrote in a
letter from Madagascar: "Modern science and
technology is nothing else than the gradual realization in practice of everything that Jules Verne
had envisioned in his books."

Jules Verne would live long enough to see some
of his dreams realized, but not those envisioned in
his latest books. These last innovations were so
incredible to his contemporaries, that they considered them technological "fairy tales." The title
of his next novel was *The Castle in the Carpath
Mountains.* In the course of its story are intro-
duced electrically-charged barbed wire and
"talking" motion pictures. Stella, a singer, unexpectedly appears to her lover on a screen and sings

him a song; he hears her voice clearly. Jules Verne elucidates on the phenomenon: "Her picture was projected on a cloth."

In another novel, *Robur the Conqueror*, which would serve as a model for many subsequent books of science fiction, he "invents" a new aerial vehicle, which he calls the Albatross. The Albatross is nothing but the modern helicopter, which the Spaniard Juan de la Gieva was to invent in 1917. In the same book, Jules Verne describes something that resembles a *sputnik*, a spherical missile that circles around the earth with tremendous speed. A sound resembling the roaring of trumpets announces its passage. Even the modern tank, the armored vehicle on traction chains, which was to speed the end of World War I in 1917, is mentioned in one of his novels.

We know that his premonitions of the destructive power of technology weighed heavily on Jules Verne when he was an old man. He gave up travel and sold his beautiful modern yacht, the *Saint Michel*, to the Prince of Montenegro. His parents had died long since. His old friend and publisher, Hetzel, was to die before the turn of the century. As Verne's circle of friends, relatives, and acquaintances became smaller and smaller every year, the number of his fans kept on increasing. But their letters and visits only disturbed him in his work. The library in the tower at Amiens now constituted the only world he wished for.

Nevertheless, there was one exception. For he loved the theater. He had never lost his youthful passion for the theater. The stage success of *Around the World in Eighty Days* and of the dramatizations of his *Captain Grant's Children* and *The Czar's Courier* meant more to him than the huge editions of his "extraordinary journeys." The world-famous author had accepted (or, rather, taken over) the position of drama critic for the little Amiens daily. The evenings spent in the theater were the only distraction from his daily routine.

He still began work at six in the morning, exactly as he had done in the beginning of his career as an author. But in the meantime he had produced more than eighty novels. He would continue writing in his study until twelve noon. After lunch he would rest for an hour, and then take a long walk with his dog, whom he had christened "Satellite" — a truly modern and scientific name. The remainder of the afternoon was spent in his very extensive library, where he would copy excerpts from the latest scientific books and add new material to his notes. He had begun his notes almost forty years earlier when he had taken refuge in the libraries of Paris as a young and unsuccessful author. By now, they comprised over 20,000 closely written pages.

His old friends appealed to his passion for the theater to lure him to Paris once again. The author attended the 500th performance of the dramatic adaptation of his successful novel *The Czar's Courier*. He sat in the seat of honor, and the public gave him a resounding ovation. A great costume ball honoring the author was given after the performance and was to last through the night.

Suddenly his friend, Felix Nadar, appeared with a reproduction of the missile in his *Journey from the Earth to the Moon*. The theme of the ball was "Journey Around the Earth." There were countless Phileas Foggs and Passepartouts in handsome costumes; others appeared as Michel Ardan, Captain Hatteras, and the engineer Cyrus Smith. The great old storyteller smilingly moved about among the characters of his novels. Upon his return to Amiens, he wrote with renewed vigor and turned out his most extravagant utopian novel, *The Diary of an American Journalist in the Year 2890*. Even today, this novel remains utopian. Once more Jules Verne had created a veritable fireworks of marvelous inventions.

In this novel, New York has become the world capital and bears the name "Universal City." Huge skyscrapers more than nine hundred feet high rise on either side of streets one hundred yards wide. Rolling sidewalks serve to speed up pedestrian traffic in the city. Only the business district is situated in the center of town; all dwellings are located in the surrounding countryside — an ideal set-up. In town, neon advertisements are projected on clouds, some of them man-made. A television set in each apartment is taken for granted, and the programs are much more varied than ours, since television programs in Universal City include reports from Mars, Jupiter, and Venus!

Universal aerial travel between the planets has long since been regulated to include all routes. Even one of the most recent inventions, the television-telephone, was foreseen by Jules Verne. This appears at times to be of dubious merit, for the subscriber can call up from the office and see exactly what is going on in every room at home. The hero of Verne's book is the editor-in-chief of the *Earth Herald*, a world-wide paper with a total circulation of eighty million.

As Jules Verne approached his seventy-fifth year, he was to experience something completely new and surprising which would make him very happy; he would see some of his visions become reality. The great World's Fair of 1900 in Paris exhibited a number of technological miracles which a few decades ago would have been considered pure fantasy. There were veritable palaces of technology. One palace was dedicated to the engineering sciences and another was devoted to mining and metallurgy. The inventors of a new era were making their debut. Two years before the turn of the century, the *Nautilus* had become a reality.

After all the historic attempts to build a submarine, John P. Holland, an Irishman, developed the first seaworthy submarine, driven by motors above water and by electric power under water. But even more important was the creation of an American, Simon Lake. It has already been mentioned that as a boy he had been an enthusiastic reader of Jules Verne's *Twenty Thousand Leagues Under the Sea.* In constructing his submarine, he had modeled it closely after the *Nautilus* and created a vessel with two hulls, placing the diving tanks and the fuel bunkers in the outer hull. Lake's submarine was also launched in 1898, and it remained the model for all larger submarines to be built until the end of World War II. This model was, as the inventor himself acknowledged, "nothing else than the perfect realization of the *Nautilus* — piece by piece."

That same year — though Jules Verne would not live to know it — a ten-year-old boy was fascinated by a book entitled *Twenty Thousand Leagues Under the Sea.* Again and again he would read the chapter in which Captain Nemo conquers the South Pole with his *Nautilus.* He made up his mind that one day he too would go there to explore the "sixth continent," as Jules Verne had called the polar region in his book. The name of this ten-year-old was Richard Evelyn Byrd, and one day he would be known as Admiral Byrd, who made history as the greatest explorer of the Antarctic.

A certain Robert E. Peary was already making preparations, in secrecy, to conquer the North Pole, which had hitherto only been reached by Captain Hatteras in a novel by Jules Verne.

The mysterious "picture box" described in *The Castle in the Carpath Mountains* had begun to rattle and click in the hands of two brothers, Louis and Auguste Lumière, who demonstrated it in a Paris suburb. It was a peculiar box showing live, swiftly moving pictures and it was given the name "Cinematographe."

And this was not all! After years of experimentation, a Dr. Rudolf Diesel realized an amazing dream — the fuel-driven engine. Already, in 1897, the newspapers were writing about the Diesel engine. There was no doubt about it, reality was beginning to catch up with Jules Verne's dreams!

8 DREAMS BECOME REALITY

THE *Lord of the World* was the title of the novel by Jules Verne published in 1903, one of his last books. In it is described a universal vehicle of the future, which could serve as a fast automobile, a submarine, and an airplane. Once more, the imagination of the seventy-five-year-old author had outstripped even the wildest plans and designs of the modern inventors.

He now devoted himself to a new book, *The Conquest of the Sea*. He already sensed that it would be his last. It revolves around a problem which would, along with the exploration of the universe, become increasingly important in the second half of our century. It deals with the utilization of the resources of the sea, which by

the early 1900's had become an urgent need, due
to the rapid growth of world population. Jules
Verne had hardly completed the book and laid
aside his pen when he became seriously ill. Early
in February he had still been able to celebrate his
seventy-seventh birthday, but by March 20, 1905,
all the newspapers carried the message that the
great storyteller was dying.

The importance of Jules Verne for his times,
and his literally world-wide fame, can be measured
by the overwhelming response to these newspaper
bulletins. The great news agencies of Europe and
America sent hourly inquiries to Amiens and published bulletins about his condition, as though it
were not an author, but the Pope or a ruler, who
lay dying.

On March 24, 1905, toward evening, Jules Verne
closed his eyes forever. During the next few days,
newspapers in all countries printed obituaries and
tributes of the sort usually accorded only to very
great statesmen. The whole diplomatic corps gathered in the cemetery of Amiens for Verne's funeral.
Among them were special envoys sent by kings
and presidents of states. The German Emperor
also sent a special delegate. Thirty members of
the French Academy attended the funeral serv-
ice, and soon afterward monuments were erected
to the memory of Jules Verne — both in Amiens
and in his native Nantes. One newspaper went so

far as to rhapsodize: "The Homer of the fifteen-year-olds has returned to the Infinite."

One of the large Paris dailies expressed the feeling of millions of readers with these sad words: "The old storyteller is dead. Is it not as though Santa Claus had died?"

From now on there would not be, twice each year, a new book by Jules Verne, packed with incredible new inventions. His complete work — almost ninety books — was finished.

And yet a few years after Jules Verne's death it would become evident that his work lived on, that even in the future it would continue to inspire inventions, and even determine the achievements of future inventors and explorers. The last great chapter of his work would be written after his death, for the visions of Jules Verne were becoming reality!

The first dream to come true was the conquest of the two Poles. First the North Pole was reached by a man who had struggled toward this goal for twenty years and who was considered the most experienced of all polar explorers, the American naval officer Robert E. Peary. In 1908 he set out on his polar expedition, accompanied by 14 Eskimos, 28 sleds, and 140 dogs. On April 6, 1909, at ten o'clock in the morning, Peary had reached his goal: The star-spangled banner was raised on the North Pole.

His triumph, in turn, became the occasion for

the conquest of the South Pole. Roald Amundsen, a Norwegian, was already on his way to the North Pole when news of Peary's success reached him. He quickly turned his ship around and headed for the South Pole.

Four decades earlier, Jules Verne described the South Pole and its conquest by Captain Nemo in *Twenty Thousand Leagues Under the Sea*. The captain sails with the *Nautilus* underneath the ice pack and hoists his black flag, with an "N" embroidered in gold, on the Pole. On December 15, 1911, a Norwegian flag was raised on the South Pole. By competing strenuously against the English expedition led by Captain Scott (that had started out much earlier), Roald Amundsen succeeded in winning the race and became the first to reach the eternal ice of the Pole. Only a month later did Captain Robert F. Scott and his exhausted companions reach the South Pole. Their disappointment at finding Amundsen's tent and the tracks made by his sleds was so great that they did not have the energy to make the return trip, and so lost their lives.

But Amundsen's triumph was not merely a stroke of good luck. Among all the works of Jules Verne, most of which were represented in his library, Amundsen had read *The Adventures of Captain Hatteras* with special attention and had made one of its basic premises his own — namely that the good preparation for a polar expedition is

half the victory. Amundsen planned his expedition
down to the smallest detail, more carefully and
thoroughly than any polar expedition before his.
Only when he had eliminated all the conceivable
sources of failure did he add his own personal
courage, his iron constitution, and his luck to the
balance.

The success of Amundsen brought a very
young American close to despair. For Richard
Evelyn Byrd had been so carried away by Captain
Nemo's trip to the South Pole that he had de-
termined, when he was ten years old, to become an
explorer and conquer the South Pole.

We know from Admiral Byrd's own words and
from his writings how much his life was influ-
enced by Jules Verne's books, and that the imagination of the great storyteller gave him the impetus to attempt his daring feats.

The "extraordinary journeys," which he had
read with ardent interest as a boy, awakened in
him such a yearning to roam through the whole
wide world that when he was twelve years old he
convinced his parents that he might travel alone
to visit acquaintances in the Philippines. But
young Byrd took advantage of the trip only to
run away. He made a tramp steamer voyage all
around the world and only came home to his
parents two years later.

In 1912, Byrd enlisted in the Navy. Because of

a foot injury he joined the Air Force in 1916, and a wholly new, magnificent world was opened up to him. Flying belonged to the future, of that he was convinced. Could he not realize his boyhood ambition in another way and conquer the Poles from the air? With energy and enthusiasm, he used his free time and evenings to study all twenty-two divisions of polar science.

The man who had, to use a slang phrase, "beat him" to the South Pole, Roald Amundsen was threatening to get ahead of him again — this time at the North Pole. In the year 1925, Amundsen began to take part in flights to the Arctic. Byrd had no doubt but that the great old explorer would be the first to fly over the North Pole.

And now there was no peace for Richard Evelyn Byrd.

In the spring of 1926, it became known that Umberto Nobile, an Italian, would enter the competition of flying over the North Pole with his airship *Norge*. Nobile would start from Spitsbergen in May. But even before the *Norge* had reached the starting point, on May 7, a small Fokker airplane almost 50 feet in length and with about a 65-foot wingspan had already arrived there. It was the *Josephine* belonging to Byrd and Floyd Bennett, his companion. Byrd's first attempt failed. But the second try was a success. On May 9, he reached the North Pole, dropped the

American flag from his plane, and returned to Spitsbergen hale and hearty fourteen hours and forty minutes after take-off.

On the evening of this memorable day, Byrd celebrated triumph together with Amundsen and the American polar explorer Lincoln Ellsworth. "Well, Byrd," Amundsen smilingly asked him as they raised their glasses in a toast, "what next?"

Without a moment's hesitation, Byrd replied: "The South Pole!"

It was a dialogue that might have come straight from a Jules Verne novel.

For two and a half years, Byrd quietly made preparations for his new enterprise; then he set out for the South Pole. When Amundsen and Scott had started out, they still went with dog sleds and without radio equipment. The airplane did not yet exist. But in 1928 Byrd appeared in the Antarctic with four boats, four airplanes, one hundred Greenland dogs and a carefully picked group of eighty-two men — the best fliers, sled drivers, sportsmen, and specialists that he could find. They founded a settlement in the eternal ice that was to become world-renowned as "Little America." It was from "Little America" that Richard Byrd started out for his new goal, the South Pole. On November 28, 1929, the motor of an airplane was heard for the first time above the sixth continent.

Byrd had to cover a total distance of about 1,700 miles, and his three-motor Fokker plane was heavily laden. He encountered a formidable obstacle in the form of a mountain barrier about 10,000 feet high blocking his path to the South Pole. Byrd had to jettison precious food supplies and even more precious gasoline in order to get over those peaks.

On November 29, shortly after one o'clock in the afternoon, he reached the South Pole, and here the American flag was thrown down by the same man who had also been the first to reach the North Pole by airplane.

In 1931, a Swiss professor, Auguste Piccard, whose adventurous personality resembled that of many a Jules Verne hero, ascended into the stratosphere in a balloon. This ascent, which had the whole world waiting in suspense, combined daring adventure with scientific exploration — the same fascinating combination that had made Jules Verne's first novel, *Five Weeks in a Balloon*, a success.

Piccard's balloon remained aloft for seventeen hours. Toward evening it began to sink, and around ten o'clock at night, in complete darkness, it floated down toward a mountain and right into a glacier. Piccard succeeded in landing his balloon on a level snow bank, and then he had to wait until daylight. The professor and his companion spent a freezing night on the glacier, and early next morning they began the arduous descent. Finally, they reached solid ground where they were met by a search party. A similar feat had already been envisioned by Jules Verne in *Five Weeks in a Balloon*. Now it had become a fact.

The same man who had been the first and only human being to rise to a height of close to 50,000 feet in a balloon was also to explore the depths of the ocean. In this case, too, he would set a new record, even though this was not his primary aim.

In January 1960, the *Trieste* reached the deepest spot on the ocean floor, it landed in the Marianas Trench in the Pacific, 11,521 meters down, thereby surpassing even Captain Nemo!

Synthetic materials were "invented" by Jules Verne many years before they were actually produced. He foresaw the manufacture of artificial diamonds (in his novel *Southern Star*). These were commercially produced for the first time just a few years ago. Verne described testing sites for atomic bombs and launching pads for space rockets.

Perhaps Jules Verne's greatest "invention" was his detailed and graphic picture of the submarine *Nautilus* in *Twenty Thousand Leagues Under the Sea*. As was pointed out before, the United States Navy felt its debt to Verne's inventiveness to be of such magnitude that it christened its first atomic submarine the *Nautilus* in honor of the author.

The memory of Jules Verne was again honored when the first launching of a manned space rocket circled the globe. And, in the future, when regular space traffic is established, Verne's readers will be reminded of the final chapters of his *Journey from the Earth to the Moon* and his *Diary of a Journalist of the Year 2850.*

As long as we shall live in an age of technology, and as long as there are daring explorations and tests to be performed that serve the cause of science, we shall remember the man who had foreseen this era in his novels.

At the outset of all the great achievements of mankind there has to be imagination. The daring and yet carefully thought-out fantasies of the great storyteller, Jules Verne, have given tremendous impetus to inventors and explorers of the age of technology. They have also aroused the interest of millions of people in the problems of technological development, the future of technology, and in scientific adventures.

Even in the future, when the entire history of technology will be recorded, Jules Verne will be remembered as "The Man Who Invented the Future."